PRAYERS FROM HEAVEN

Volume 2

With Love,
Peter A. Boice

PETER BOICE

ISBN 979-8-88832-994-8 (paperback)
ISBN 979-8-88832-996-2 (hardcover)
ISBN 979-8-88832-995-5 (digital)

Copyright © 2024 by Peter Boice

All rights reserved. No part of this publication may be reproduced, distributed, or transmitted in any form or by any means, including photocopying, recording, or other electronic or mechanical methods without the prior written permission of the publisher. For permission requests, solicit the publisher via the address below.

Christian Faith Publishing
832 Park Avenue
Meadville, PA 16335
www.christianfaithpublishing.com

Printed in the United States of America

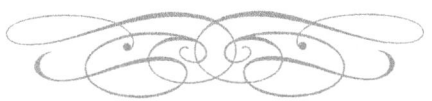

Introduction

These inspired writings come from the hearts of a devote Christian. They express wonderous love and exuberant praise of the Lord. These religious essays have joyous religious fervor and reveal the passionate nature of a true believer. The passage of the writings is dazzling in their worship of the perfect Being, in his wisdom and goodness. We are urged to trust in his love for all. The strong faith that shines forth in these writings are like a Book of Life.

The strong faith that shines forth in these writings show a spirit that has been elevated to embrace God to the highest degree. They also show a fervent and humble spirit. The reader finds freshness and pure joy expressed in these writings. The writings and their messages are very clear and are of a strong affirmation in the life of the believer.

Just as the resurrection proved us right in Him, so the reason to look into these writings is to improve one's relationship with Jesus and the Godhead, time and again from his journey, it is the same Jesus and Trinity, just a little more robustly given.

Preface

He was saved at age thirty-six.
He still writes at age seventy.
He is a Pentecostal Catholic of faith.
Each day, he worships Jesus through the Holy Spirit. Each day is an inspiration through the Holy Spirit.

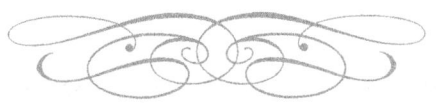

God's Mercy

The coming together after a misery is key to lasting relationships.

The absolute care for one another shows the legacy the one who passed away leaves with the living.

Having impartial review of the loss and what is leftover, reviewing of less the understood becomes better.

For one, not to be misled, a detached view of life continues even after a loss.

Sometimes, it can mean a radical reappraisal of people and motives they, at first, were assumed to have.

People should avoid bearing snap decisions.

Changed, Not Lost

A benediction heals the community, putting it on a new footing of faith with the Lord. It better looks like His Agape Love. All become messengers of this new grace.

It is a summation of a hero's life. The charity and love are on display. The prayers for heaven are brought forth. All recall their meeting and the holy ground they stood on. And how holy ground moves to a newer reality of lovers.

We are into a lot of red tape with memories.

Newer faces pick up friendship. We are all together, even the one lost.

Now in the Spirit.

Repentant Sinners

The hope in the Holy Spirit is spectacular; it is our curious nature amplified. Our nature is satisfied within Him because He leads us to Jesus. With Him, our faith and love are aflame for Jesus. It is Agape.

Listen and the Way will reveal itself. If we notice, He calls on many levels. His word resounds on us.

The Gospel of Jesus portrayed in the Bible is the Agape version, which believers aim to live by. There are strongholds in us we have not found. We are likely to repent for them. We may not know them, but the Holy Spirit will indicate them.

His Coming Together

The Lord, risen from all complexities, offered sacrifice for ours. God granting forgiveness gives us freedom from all our complexities when we are absolute in Jesus. Trust like this cannot be backed off from.

The merging of souls indicates that the wills are exact. My will is not exact for productiveness. It searches.

Without thinking, things fall into place. And when they do, we realize it was perfect.

The extent of forefront remains an unfixed notion. In many circles, it is atmospheric related.

The calm is very suggestive. The patience is rewarded by contemplation heart to heart.

The Faithful

God raises His Triune nature in high worship.
God blesses all to Grace.
In the doing of Life, we come to see wishes shared by all. There, there is:

> Jehovah niche.
> Jehovah jico.

What will come pleases both necessity and want.
Impossible Faith is God. For the Just, He lives on such faith. That is His trust.
We, overcomers, come firsthand to this impossible faith. That is His sovereignty.
And we are in sovereign covenant. Jesus.
So for us, His song is Joy.

Prayerful Insight, Worship Healing

With worship comes the insight. Experience is all worship insight.
Worship trains the mind and heart to the word. It reveals the anointed word. And the anointed gift, to be exposed for fulfilling the way.
The tempo of music drives home to the spirit was what necessary gifting to surmount a challenge of grace in God's sovereignty.
The high worship ends all pleasure to His overcoming.
The mind-heart connection is high worship. There, the soul is offered to God in Faith as a Trust.

Impossibly So, Grace Raises Up Us Children

We see a pathway of Truth. It shows how He made it all possible.

The Agape Love converts one to His Word.

The Agape worship heals one to discipleship. The gifts of the Spirit are there, waiting for a word.

The immersion of the song into one is a key to stepping forward. One does not step up but have intimacy reveal greater extents of grace with God.

Prayer is the life of the believer in concert with Agape.

Traveling with Christ

I can only say things are well when I admit the truth.

Life is a wonder. We may err, only to correct ourselves.

Jesus has all marvels planned out if we just rest in Him, with thanksgiving and praise. Discuss the truth.

Take time to record His works. In faith, we travel in Christ in love and joy, His realized perfection (in us).

You may wonder why He doesn't shoulder more activity. He is raising a fold of cousins. We are one in Him.

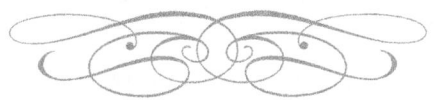

My Challenge

There are challenges to the believer. But none are as difficult as one. Are you authentic?

The fruit of the tree you have tells the story. The fruit of indifference tells of the corruption.

The ridicule corruption presents is a shaming of the gospel crucifixion. The flesh has overtaken. Only the worship of His Name can restore the believer's overtaking of the world.

This overcoming of this world has a God moment for the world's flesh. It is an open joy to behold.

My hope is that all will come to an honest belief like this.

Son of the Living God

The word shifts in us.
It is our light to the Gospel.
Abortion is the choice of intercourse.
Prayer sings with His Heart.
We are authentic to the kingdom of God.
Our weapons are the grace of God.
The Holy Spirit meets us over. To Him, all Faith ascribe. Love purposes us in Him:
The boisterous Live Jesus Christ.

The Land of Jesus

You go through life and see the distortions of life. The constant drag to draw you back is of the flesh. The Land of God is a constant discernment of the evidence of the Holy Spirit, the Spirit of Truth.

The Land of Jesus is keeping the love Agape and reaching out with Grace.

What is not pure as love needs care.

It is God's way of pointing out a challenge.

Faith is necessary as a trust between you and the Maker. The Holy Spirit is there with Jesus's person. The more we discern His life, the more we grow.

Graceful Living

Our goal is freedom under the Lord Jesus Christ. He is our authority with the power of the Holy Spirit. Under God the Father's guidance, we give freedom its authority.

In this freedom, we have the art over women's activities and the authority over man's activities comparing the whole social fabric. Like a welcome tapestry is the whole of this fabric under the freedom of Jesus Christ.

We thank God for this insight into His doings.

The faithful are drawn into holy imitation of His highest character, Grace.

Grace on the Way

Words fail to describe the transfiguration.

Change came Pentecost Sunday when the believers were transfigured with tongues resting on them. They could only speak of the marvel of Jesus Christ, risen from the grave. Transfiguring allows what is in God's interest to come forth. Jesus, Moses, and Elijah were dazzling before the chosen disciples. They earmark when now all He will contend with is grace to complete the law and the prophets in love.

From the burning tongues will come the great evangelism. The confession that Jesus Christ is the Son of the Living God. This continues to today with our confession of faith.

Resting

We are complete in Him.
His sacrifice takes all with Him.
In Him, we are complete. The Divine Father shares all of us with Jesus. We are all a part of a whole. The complete has come. The partial moves away, transformed.
The Holy Spirit is our meeting ground in Him. The Word is made afresh and renewed. The Song of Christ is complete within us, Jesus.
The stigma is on our word overcomer.
The gifting is in us. God's transliteration of the Word in us.

Completely His

The Lord God Almighty has complete control over all by graces. It is all supernatural, miracles abound.
We have no clue to the full depth of Christ's result as a sacrifice. Only that He satisfies freedom of sins. Since His power to bless us omnipotent. What else than restoration of the kingdom?
Oh, yes. Uh, hum, worship in Jesus completes us.
All those giftings become available through grace. Amen to Jesus. You my Love.
I am yours.
You are a holy nation, a royal priesthood. Jesus, you're forever.
In the sacrifice of Jesus, all His are made complete.

It Is Done

Fortunately for us who believe the Paraclete in our prayers' exciting faith. There is no better helper. If we listen to Him, Jesus will come alive.

Have we surrendered to God? He waits.

If we want to deepen our regard for Him, surrender to God, now.

The response is the open holy of holies is God. Your brother Jesus Christ.

You worship Him and reveal your anxiety.

It is done.

Believe and thank Him. It takes a special time to reveal the supernatural to the natural. Have faith in a loving God.

Our Savior

The Lord's Prayer is a prayer of love to your Creator.
The salutation we give each other is a prayer of well-being.
We promise to follow Him by such prayers of love.
Each time we pray to the Lord, we are recommissioned.

Talking to each other is useless unless we personalize it. It is then that the Personable Lord can flow in our discussions.

After all of science and technology, we still have biblical notions of the mind and heart.

Abiding with God remains in us. God always keeps our betterment if we rest in Him.

Jesus Is Lord

Jesus is the Light from the Father, the way of Salvation. He is incarnate to us. We are His people, the fruit of the Vine.

We are empowered by the Holy Spirit for Church. The succession of the apostles is in our faith. Our giftedness has yet to be fully realized through the Holy Spirit. All the gifts of the Spirit are realized in His Church, the kingdom of God. The perfection of Christ is upon us. We are freed to holiness under Christ. We are set free from the bondage of sin and of the lowly grace. We have a discerning intuition that keeps us grace-led.

Heaven is real to us as new creations in His Blood.

You Need Overflowing Love

He loves the indiscreet because they open possibility thinking. And the use of faith expends.

As we pray, we interrupt the Lord.

Alleluia.

The use of grace is to enliven souls and stretch hearts.

His Grace of Love is to counter the power of sin. We do not know what it is to cause others to sin; demonic battles of the mind take over. It is not worship.

And the flesh will show in the heart in areas of shame, blame, and guilt over competition, not Gospel.

He Sees All

The joy of the Lord is coupled with the warrior of God.

The armor of God is upon the godly man with discernment.

The love of God is all we are.

The life of God is all of us.

We are guided people to have the love of Jesus shine and for people see the Christ. We are the people of Jesus Christ. Very true.

We are His prayer, a proven work of grace. Now He wants to see how much of that grace can be returned with the end of sin.

He knows who will make it through with the Father, Son, Spirit, grace, many. But God Almighty sees all of us differently, overcomers.

Yes, God sees all.

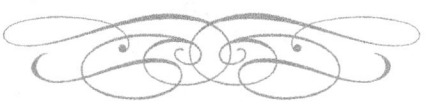

Loving with God

Living with His Spirit is acting in consciousness with His life. Being a spiritual man is not easy. It is a battle with the flesh. It seeks redemption under; it is made to suffer in the cross.

The result of walking with the Lord to heal memories is a righted suffering with Him.

Each suffered healing is a redemption of the memory into graces. The Lord God wants the most erroneous fulfilled.

Begin confessing God's actions. Then give yourself up with God.

Make sure your gift of love is adequate with His Agape of love.

Accepting Him

Get inspiration from on high worship. The form must appeal to your calling Jesus.

Authentically, calling means you no longer appeal but request. The trust is there already. He is shepherding.

Having His Presence, praise and praise.

Give Him the reason for being your Savior.

As you find, He is yours. Rest in Him.

Be as one in Him. Fruit of the Spirit be with you.

The overtaking love is yours. The love of the Lord is with you.

Lost and He Prays for Grace

I see the insight of God everywhere. Honestly, He is searching all of us.

Grace is justly executed. The measure of grace is holiness unto God. And repeated to have results beyond the senses.

He wants to see how weak we are in grace and how focused we are in Him. So He invites HS inspiration. He wants to recover fruit of the Spirit and see if we are ready for Him.

Jesus has our truth.

He knows we are challenged. But is grace aligned to Him? Then the fruit of the Spirit will showcase in Him.

Otherwise, we are in our flesh and must seek Him, God.

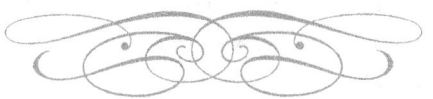

Knowing God

Whether we are in a group or alone, the Paschal mystery plays alive with us.

Forever the mystery remains with us to the ends of the Word. It is in Him we seek our purpose. The glory of His Presence puts us at His bounds of persona. The oneness of Him ties us with Him in glory. There He capitulates with us in person.

Worship reveals us to His Holy core, His holy of holies.

Love is the agent grace to beholden as Agape, now and forever.

As long as man worships, we shall know.

Deus Abba

Toward our brokenness, we find Him, alive and pure.

In Him, the name flourishes. He is Father to all.

We lift our praises and worship to Him, forever.

The Word shapes our thought life in spirit to salvation.

My Papa is God Almighty. His identity is Jesus Christ.

He defeated the world, the flesh, and the devil.

He is Risen with our corpus delicti. So we are in Him in praise and worship.

Albeit as we know him intimately, He is still in the beyond.

Only He Knows the Time

Our aging poses a question. Are we comfortable with anymore change with life?

It's like broken glass. How much more broken are we before we change? Or have we already gone broken?

The Bible stands for lives broken into victory.

Keep faith and miracles will occur. And we are, too, for the comfort of good souls.

We are being blessed. Our time is coming. And we are gleaning the very good out of life. Redemption coming over allows experiences. Character is prevalent. Friendships echo the family of God to us. We are common and very blessed.

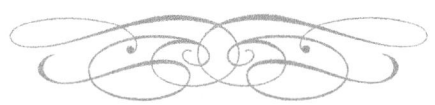

Celebrate Jesus, Be Whole

Savior talk. The celebrations of the family.
The family is a blessing.
Be in touch. God grants special graces. Find and be blessed. The Spirit of God heightens our resolve for family.
Look at the Gospel. We all are repentant sinners. We all are. We are familiar. He knows.
And we do too.
The blessed stand forth as God's kingdom, all of us. We are praised to His Coming. And we are going.
Praise be to Jesus.
What it is we want? A loving true God. Find Jesus.

The Family of God

My sister and her family are my family. The family of God. Michigan and South Carolina hold my cousins with a few scatterings. God blesses them all.
It's a walk of grace to see how we are ultimately all related to each other. The branches of my family in God are Americans. They each enjoy our freedoms with great reward.
That is humankind, all so different in the reward of freedom.
It is our character that is formed, a politics of necessity. A very brief way to each other—that is our freedom to each. And a sign of our own development.

Free at Last

As we mature, we notice changes. It leads us into a quagmire of sorts when authority is applied to change.

The struggle in the leadership and within, we remark how volatile it is when change comes.

Keeping steadfast and visionary is remarkable. With Jesus, it's a walk of grace Agape. With people and their scruples, its putting all within a microscope. The Spirit of Truth eliminates all introversion when we accept Jesus. He is whole to me, not a particle-by-particle look. His bridging across issues is a leading of miraculous faith grace.

He is holy, and we are to image Him.

Gospel Healing

In the Gospel, shame, blame, and competition are gone. In the kingdom, language is the evidence of acceptance, Freedom.

Illness and diseases test the trust of each acceptance. Only oneness with God restores it.

Freedom is God in one's life to do the impossible wish, maintenance.

The impossible, us, is to find a way with God's blessing. If injury surmounts one, then remedy is larger than life, Jesus.

He spells people to their wishes. Unbroken trust He keeps through mutuality. The growing of respect signals truth.

Everything Matters

To have faith in Jesus is to know He is a reasonable Lord. Magnification of Almighty God. He is a wondrous Miracle Maker.

He leads us into His kingdom. We see the families. We are interwoven by graces of love. It forces us to be prayerful in our acceptance of other's graces.

The areas of our heart find His favor through those same graces. We develop personally. Our leading edge is agape, full of forgiveness and mercy. We abide to His Gospel of reconciliation.

Friendships take a gravity of meaning, each according to their fullness in Christ and the life of Jesus.

The Risen Lord, Our Way

His overcoming we share explicitly in all events realizing victory with Him.

Being empathic over time helps us to victory in grace. There, His unseen force supplants. We only need the will and direction. Thank You, Holy Spirit.

Whether it is in service or inspired indwelling, the Holy Spirit recognizes Jesus through us. It is victory of uplifted faith.

Larger-than-life high worship directs us to truths within Jesus that endear us to Him and to others.

His, being perfect giving, makes our surrender approaches to Him more palatable and real.

The Promising Age

The time of our age is full of grace, respect, and honor. The love for each other and the honor we keep is one of a kind.

We are a blood of graces. And the Spirit abides well with me. We have a touch of heaven here.

No one is anyone's Babylon. We are our own martyr. The Lord manages all. It is an art of faith and mutual kindness. The sheer kindness to this place brings a hope imperishable to each heart. We are part of God's kingdom that has earned its due of praise and reward from God.

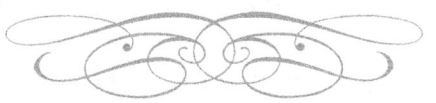

Complete Surrender– Baptism of the Spirit

That darkness will test you; it is inevitable. How well we cling to Him is not clear.

The Holy Spirit is our helper to secure relationship. He guides us through baptism and to a closer walk with Jesus when we repent and go forward in believing Jesus is the Son of God.

We have groanings that come through the Spirit to God, indicating our essential needs and praise to Jesus. They are the fruits of being reborn or baptized in the Spirit. It is affected by prayer spontaneously or over time.

Final Transformation

My thinking is that mature-practicing Christians have crossed over the baptism of the Holy Spirit.

He comforts us over God's control and the end times.

He points to Jesus and reminds us of salvic grace through Jesus. He ushers us in through the spiritual life to the gates of the kingdom.

Graces endow us with charisma for the pleasure of the Holy Spirit and Jesus. We become a living stone of faith in the church of Jesus Christ.

Let Him Shine

An active prayer life and intimate worship of God are the signs of healthy service in one.

The robust faith in Jesus keeps one steady in the up-and-down nature of this life. That is the purpose of the Holy Spirit baptism. That ripe connection with His Spirit keeps me healthy in the kingdom.

It's a "God bless" when you stay well within the kingdom of God. He never fails.

Politics aside because Truth bears witness to God's Way. Be gospel and love Jesus Agape. He never stops loving you.

When Jesus Shines

Our God can read our spirits and our hearts and souls, our very movements of life.

Our moms and dads are with the Eternal Father and Jesus, praying for us. It's all done on a supernatural level. Your hopes and wishes are before Jesus Christ through the groans of the Spirit. These are different than the gift of tongue, another supernatural language. It is a charism of the Holy Spirit, for those in prayer of the baptism of the Holy Spirit. The gifts of the HS, or charismata, are opened by faith. The most common one is the gift of helps. One can be baptized so with fervent prayer. An active prayer life is a sign of the Holy Spirit and His baptism. An active life with Him is all it takes, a gospel life. Honoring God is all it takes. Selflessness is the sign of Jesus.

Look Onward and Up

Yes, you are part of the holy, God be with you. You are the breath of salvation. Call your Lord and God and make special marks of faith to draw His Person into the light of all. Pray you can share in grace with the undeserving and make a holy friend.

Waiting on the Lord Jesus is wishing for His reconciliation with the Father to consider well those in right standing through the Son and Spirit

Measures well the grace that bears your name and how nothing is all you are to His everything.

Feel His energy. Consuming wrath. Opening the heavens. Jesus ablaze with the Father, sonship of grace. We wait. The everlasting Spirit douses our soul with charismata, we find the trust of father.

Belief Is a Paschal Mystery, Jesus

The Paschal mystery is all of Christ.
He is Jesus heaven sent. The One who heals.
See us form together, worship the truth. All saints recall the grace of salvation. We are revelation history of Him.
Our line is when we knew Him first, and we surrendered our offering.
High worship always raises Him into view. We celebrate all of God. We are sunk in His travels with us, redemption.
The Paschal mystery we all play a part in His revelation.

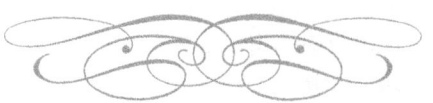

Healing Me

We, his faithful, hear His call in our desert.

The terrain of our conscience is difficult, but with the added weight of the heart, the inspiring gets through. Circumstances play the role of heightening emotions.

The combined graces in our life challenge us. We are battling. The graces of the Lord heal me. I recognize the Holy Spirit. Now Jesus is revealed. It is He alone who musters me into a new creation. He is now God to me.

My soul parks up to Him within, about and above. Now I am of age, with the Father, God Eternal.

Finding His Passion

Don't be peers with your laurels, have a hunger, a passion, undefiable. Don't you think God is crafting you for absolute surrender? To be as Jesus to do something utterly contrary to human nature? We are stunned how our world fails before our very eyes. Are you a catalyst for reform, enlightened illumination? Are you the key that will unlock the door for sinners to repent and seek redemption? You are! At best, we are repentant sinners, however engrained the sin is, not beyond prayer and grace.

So you cross out for deeper surrender? Don't let your comfort overwhelm you. Be a living grace, a living prayer. Walking the steps of God in His blessed will. Shine! Ask God what He wants of you. There is time for more and greater.

God's Wisdom

The Spirit of God cries out:
Jehovah niche.
Jehovah jiro.
God will supply our needs and wants.
We are a people who depend on the inspiration for life.
Kingdom walk is not without its challenges.
The Flesh has got to be nailed to our cross.
Let the Holy Spirit have freedom over us.
With the Word comes our resolve to do God's work on time.
We are a holy nation of believers who overcome.

Thank You, Lord

God says the time is ripe. He puts the means together. Our love for Him. So He puts us intimate to Him, and grace belies us. We follow His start little thinking He has already put us together, little He started all and not our choice.

He is pleased we chose a better path, intimacy.
There is a rest for us to ponder.
Our song is a perpetual shepherding us to freedom.
He puts us to challenge our faith. So their trust for the Cross… and freedom in His blood and water. Are His signs too overcoming?

Yes, they should overcome any doubt that He is the Risen Lord God Almighty.

Miracle Time

God is here when relatives write. We offer ourselves in innocence. Never do we expect hurt, when we say "hi." Just a shower of graciousness.

When we go somewhere, it is family. When with others, grace be yours. We love you, all of our family, evermore.

God alone. Family alone. People keep each other.

Freedom to the soul means acceptance and the light of grace. Family members seek this, even with impoverished ways. It is all possible through God.

Have we prayed for someone? A living prayer for God to intervene.

It all is miracle work, our heart in His hands.

The Lamb Takes All Families

You give up the obvious for lasting peace and grace.
Smile. His family lives. Interior pleasure is God's favor.
Son of the Living God shines the true gospel. We live it to death.
Our teeming memories slur God's promises. And we look to our displeasure and not to His pleasure.
We were given life to His pleasure. In us is the seed to ours.
We need each to His acknowledgement. He has order for victory in our lives. We bless each other when we say "hi." Today, we go forth in the charm of His grace, spreading the news of His reconciliation, Jesus Christ.

God in Glory

The favored live to represent the rest of us. We are their living icons. Together, we are family. Some more desperately cling to the old.

Forgiven and loved is the old, family. Some old are shortsighted others have macro vision. It is family.

The family of God is all perceptions of us.

You live to breathe the same air. He loves and redeems, breathes the same air.

His breath is the same as ours. The holy ones come along as us. We are their kin, a worship of the truth of Jesus the Christ.

The Healing

The family of God is love and forgiveness.

They are there to forget, and there is no reason for it. Time moves us on.

There seems to be more urgent than this—selfish love—not Agape on bold.

We are shaped early on. On us we decide how to mold ourselves.

Likely, these are both faces. Our tastes and pleasures are caught up in the Agape of the Living God. We let live and let God.

Behold the Lamb of God who takes away my sin. He is my brother.

Wonderful

The absolute surrender is due to our invested celebration of Jesus Christ.

Jesus Christ's homage and praise is daily.

What a joy it is to know you have given it all over to Him. Inspiring trust, yes.

The power of the cross and of the Risen Lord, yes.

He has overcoming power, and I am risen beyond mere circumstance to a heavenly abode of grace. Thank You, God. And so it is a song of the heart we get lost in, wonderful freedom.

So overcome and smitten by Agape Love, all God. Radiant and true. We have into Him.

He remains patient and true, forgiving, and loving.

We Need Your Presence

These united states are a unrehearsed shell games of emotion. It just takes one to be a lightning rod to gather under pressure.

We as a people listen to disinformation daily. Tear down the lightning rods and cancel the shell games for the honest truth that government is a bias. Only the need/want of people counts.

It takes courage to get order put together. Another party to deflect the negative grace.

What is conservative/liberal, right/progressive,
One, holy spirited, is a must.

Lost and He Prays for Grace

I see the insight of God everywhere. Honestly, He is searching all of us.

Grace is justly executed. The measure of grace is holiness unto God. And repeated to have results beyond the senses.

He wants to see how weak we are in grace and how focused we are in Him. So He invites HS inspiration. He wants us to recover fruit of the Spirit and see if we are ready for Him.

Jesus has our truth.

He knows we are challenged. But is grace aligned to Him? Then the fruit of the Spirit will showcase in Him.

Otherwise, we are in our flesh and must seek Him, God.

Almighty

The light of Jesus. So emancipating. Freedom in the Spirit. His relationship. His abiding. Perfecting graces.

Jesus, Son of the Living God.
Challenges and Repentance.
I belong.
Light burning off the dross.
The holy baptism.
Oneness.
He speaks through writing.
He is all in all by way of the Spirit.
He waits for recognition as your love.
Sweet Jesus Christ. Love of all lovers.

The Holy Spirit is among us. He that grace is resurrection. For us and for all time, God.

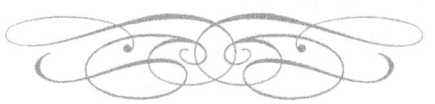

All Shadows Gone in the Light

The old memories always stir within me. The times at school, the myriad odysseys. The incomplete character. A melding pot of life. Then the end and the beginning of all, the time of my awakening.

Jesus, always present but not personal.

He is the One. The Helper is incredible. God the Father.

Born for worship.

A man of God, intimate. Healing wounds for His glorification. A new creature.

One with Him.

All the People

The birth of our country and all military days we reserve for abortion.

Our freedom is so rewritten up and to be in our legal documents.

We set the tone for individual rights, like alcohol and abortion. We reserve the right to correct prior legal decisions.

Now, in some states, rights consider the intercourse of people as sacred act. Our freedoms are not all universal. Each state is messenger. And we keep all uniquely blooded, like the people.

God Was Unexplained

The unexplainable was the heart. It ruled me unconsciously.

I learned my social behaviors in the quiet. This would talk to me unimpeded. It was a talk that I was safe in the quiet. That all the answers were in the quiet of one distraction.

The quiet distractions made me a great listener but not a great talker. I was very mill in social circles.

The quiet would have voices that I would simply manage. There was basic enlightenment. God was present. I knew Him in an instinctive way. My time had not come, for years.

It Was His Heart of Pain I Knew

My grace was a saving one. One which kept me content and as a companion. For years, it would be so until at twenty-one in a car with my folks I uttered, "Can I speak now?"

My years in quietude were broken by art in a mental institute.

My utterings would reveal a great hurt. It was a pain I carried in the quiet of God.

Until I knew Him, only this quiet would be.

The quiet of the Lord was a way for Him to be and not so.

Serendipity, What Interests Me about Reality

It is His serendipity of presence we follow.
Extraneous wordings may proceed and may follow what the spirit groans.
To initiate this one, just have an unfounded hope that things will get better, things will get better explained, or I will explain what's tugging on my heart. My dad couldn't explain it nor could mother. It left me in the quiet.
I could only listen to myself, which was being speechless.
I found the courage to speak when I no longer waited on them for attention.

The Gaining Spirit

Wisdom calls us to wait on the Lord for His directions. The voice of the quiet grace shifts as the serendipity forms graces.
The serendipity is God's mercy on our circumstances. In the quiet, it forms the grace line we are intended for.
God in the quiet has inspired our heart with potency and direction for a godly path for one to follow with one's graces on God.
Revealing the true nature of abiding is what worship does for our heart.

Rising Serendipity of Present Graces

Once we can determine His Grace, we know how to follow Him. This takes the practice of answering to His grace and its invitation by our heart strings.

It takes practice listening for Him in the quiet.

We recall our words and body respond to our heart and His gracious invite.

In a temporal ease, we accept His call.

And amuse it for furthermore. The grace only needs simple responses. Then it employs serendipity. Yes, the grace of God discerns. It is a living call from a Living God.

He calls our inner man more deeply, to engage its graces to the Risen Lord Jesus with rising graces.

His Grace Is upon Us

All that shows is that grace is forever present. The arm of the Lord is forever present with serendipity. We just have to match up. And the inspiration of the Holy Spirit does the job.

It is fortuities. We can only say we were present when the Lord arose.

It all takes for the HS to work is a set circumstance with conflict and some mercy involved. The heart of God is always looking at the natural and where God can intervene. It responds to our inner heart with faith. God first loves me so. When we do recognize faith out of God, we tell love is imparted. And mercy.

Faith: The Constancy of the Lord

The makings of the Lord are the ways faith is born within the believer.

As a grace, it is within the atmosphere one lives. This lived atmosphere relates to our senses. It means to be evident in the natural, faith.

As we determine faith exists for us, we find a curiosity where it leads. Our atmosphere becomes our reality where we come to terms of it by our thinking. Our emotions play a role in our thinking as to what is pleasurable.

And with constancy of thought, we attack a role for faith. And with faith we witness God.

Chance Grace

Then Lord sees all our doings and inspires according to what He sees should happen.

His vision is prophetic. It also shows mercy with His grace.

We are never at a lack. We are in the abundant life.

Where we miss is our myopic vision and not being patient resting in the Spirit. There are our godly choices.

If we find the ways of Him, we become overcomers.

It is simply finding how well suited we are with His inspiring. And finding the serendipity.

Receive Him/Overcome/Alleluia

Do you think the foolishness in the Spirit is superior to all our thinking that is so superior? Do we see our loving as His is Agape? Do we wish for our loving to be Agape as the love command and the loving commandment are? Certainly, we want to love Him Agape and to love our neighbor and ourselves as Agape. Is not this Agape the fruit of the Spirit? Or do we find better our way of loving, like we must then find our way of decision-making superior to His?

To have Agape in our decisions and loving, we need a baptism of the Holy Spirit. Surrender and receive.

Seeing and Loving

Do we see all as life or not? Do we see Him loving all we choose or all we love? Do we love to do all we do, or does love be Agape? Is God Agape? Do we find us loving through Him Agape? What does He want to see through us? Does He want to see through us and extension of Him or through us our decision-making? Does He want us to abide ultimately with Him as Agape or a decision to abide? Does the choice of Him allow our love to be Agape? Do we wish for it to be? Do we surrender when we love Him? Should we love Him Agape? Should we see through His eyes the life we have?

From Death to Life

Your love has carried me. Lord Jesus has kept me safe within His arms and wishes the same for you. Up to the time of reckoning.

At your time of reckoning, He will become God to you. And His presence will be heaven, not simply contentment or peace. His heaven will become heaven for you. And He will be your personal Savior.

Kingdom steps will become apparent to you—forgiveness, mercy, and grace. Then you will be charismatic, baptized in water and fire. Then you shall know Him. You are in Him, and He is in you. As you are His, His is you by prayer of each. Yes, I love You, Jesus.

A Live Experience

The use of these writings is to look into the heart and soul of a believer. A set freedom.

All grace and comeliness are in one baptized in the fire, charismatic.

The New World is in his eyes. Gone is the longing. Jesus Christ is here, the Lamb.

The lamb of God is the Way. The love is alive in the Resurrected One. He praises Abba.

With a broken and contrite heart, he comes to the Lord Jesus.

The Lamb is victorious.

Discerning

Holy discernment comes when one is in gospel reaching for beyond the charismata. Gifting and excessive reaching make the discerning to one active holiness.

One needs to be off. Complete cool. Then discerning follows charism-gifting. Let there be adequate means of the gospel. Be in love with God Jesus. Follow the inspiration of the Holy Spirit. Be one in Him, God reborn.

Let intuition guide with the Holy Spirit. Pure Gospel.

Find your source. Plug in and get real.

Be creative in ideas of revelation, all lead to Christ. We have a Lamb champion, Risen Lord, once for all time supreme sacrifice.

Mend with Grace

To do the will of God is to hear us say, "I can do it." He is omnipresent. In any action of our motivation, He is.

All we do in Him is a faith contrast, complete or incomplete.

With anything in faith, it is perpetual growth.

I am always growing in the kingdom. All aspects of pure faith are His. It is character building, of our past, not of fleshy past, incomplete, but of not finished past.

The rest or the peace you have after this comes with the graces found and ended so. We look past for graces not so now or suggested.

Seduction by Key Graced

Yes, the spirit is being seduced by supernatural graces. It involves stepping back to access the nature of the compliance.

But a leap of faith, going beyond one's reach involves truth and trust. That is the sold-out fanatic. Always pointed to grace and deliverance. One is in charge of these graces which reside in our acceptance of truth by the Holy Spirit. It knows us and our desires in spiritual life and our tested limits of responsibility and trust, the limit our discernment will allow.

Just in Time

In the faith of the believer comes the matching repentance to the Gospel from one's own.

The misalignment of faith in relations makes healing cross over biblical ways.

People panic at competition. They lose faith and trust.

Goal setting thrives with honorable pursuits. The matching of ego trusts is vital to faith and truth.

This being with Jesus is healing. Being so is faith. Overcoming faith.

Move mountains with your faith. The way is clear for your kingdom stepping; be with faith.

The Next Step in Holiness

In the midst of relationship comes the challenge to continue and deepen graces wholeness. It is how we recognize the moving graces in our field of play. Timing manages. As we see the developing field of play, we glimpse into a macro view of things at play.

The grace of God in His kingdom, not meant for only His triune nature, but also the heavenly host. It is revealed in covenant to us. His brothers and sisters see mercy of His forgiveness, kingdom stepping. It is faith pursuing the impossible and reaching it. Our age is determined by eternal principles, stepping beyond one's comfort to challenge grace and trust.

This is finding the frontiers with God. And to find if it hears your need, pray. And discern if it satisfies your emptiness and fills your need.

Command So

The Lord commands His mystery be spread far and wide. The mystery is His Son Jesus.

The magisterium of Jesus is His Father God and the firmament of heaven, the heavenly host of saints.

The levels of trust are indigenous how the base of freedom inaugurates trust.

The way of grace is to ensure trust.

Truth is a slant of real life. Divide and have people be underdeveloped.

The revealed in broken trusts feed on their own. Recasting relationships is the development of forgiveness, personal.

The trick of democracy is making it real.

Love Revered

I remember the glory of the Lord Jesus. He stood on the heart mountain and declared the Word of freedom, His name. All was given over to Him. In the consent of prayerful hands on me, the Holy Spirit became one in me.

Yeshua upon me.

The day was upon me. I immersed a word. All was done.

Out of the shadow of my grave, I came to Jesus.

I was made an apostle, a disciple, born free.

The generous light of the Holy Spirit overtook me. Catholic, forever his.

The Touch

The touch of God is complemented by a broken or contrite heart. Then He begins within me.

The will of our favor to God is upon us.

Love with faith of us is in us as hope. That holy hope we land within Him as loving-faithfulness, to Jesus, Son of the Living God.

Our life is called to reveal our wealth of the Book, His Word.

Our activity is according to the revelation we consent to of His Son. To abide, gifted by His Holy Spirit carves a special desire for us to please Him.

A Resurrected Spirit Ends Sin's Dominance

Touching God heals the mind/heart relation to a new spirit within His. In Him, all Spirit dwells, Jesus.

Jesus Christ is the summation of overcoming grace to the law. The senses get undercut by the flesh. The truth of Jesus reduces the flesh. The senses are freed and grace is buoyed. The Spirit floats beyond.

Our conscience is relieved of sin. Our steady worship reveals the Christ among us. We are entities of grace. The burden of sin/death is no more. We are enlightened to Jesus.

At the Foothills of Greatness

The shining of His heart is on everyone.

My touch and His form love. Dying is the old spirit. Heaven is upon us. The kingdom of God flourishes in His name. I live beside Him, breathing His breath.

There, in us, is hope magnified by His being. The Holy Spirit takes us on His shoulders and gives us a birth in the heavenly hosts of God.

We walk His way, past death to resurrected life.

His heart shines in us.

We move our ages into uncharted areas. The faith of God shines a pathway for us.

The Irrevocable

With blind faith, we are proceeded with God's grace, sealed in the blood. The miracle of being with Him is every day.

The Lord God Almighty Jesus Christ shows the kingdom to all related by faith in Him. They know they take kingdom steps when things beyond reach are graced.

This is the way of God, to make the believer real. He is an overcomer. And He treats all our challengers. We become overcomers.

We worship Him and place Him by faith. As we grow, we decide His way, to be pleased with a living trust.

In Grace

We look for assurance. Faithfulness in His character, a covenant promise.

As the day moves forward, so my need for divine intervention increases. His grace illuminates our decisions. We make more challenges, although they seem very normal. We are one higher plane. Our graces are matching. Our rest is well within. Our love within Him is more prominent to worship. It is thankful, our discerning registers.

In caring for His needs across people, the Spirit gifts us to together, a church of His.

The Blood Covenant

The blood of Christ is the apostolic succession through the Unity of the Holy Spirit, Jesus.

Jesus comes through for the minions. He acts in concert with His father's wishes in Christ. And so proceeded him to Jesus.

He brings us through the triumphal gate. The gate to heaven. Heaven awaits.

The King Jesus has the rule, and we are blessed.

We carry our cross to oblivion. Christ gathers even before then. In His words, we exclaim faith. His words are gentile and true. They offer us brotherhood.

His

Authentic, real unto Jesus Christ, a disciple of His we are.

In His grace, we are sufficient. And because of Him as an overcomer. He loves prior to ours. Now and forever, we love.

We love to know each other. We love to live with each. We love because He made us. We love because He is love. Because He loved us to love. Filled with love, we become love.

All graces are ours. All mercy is ours. All forgiveness is ours. All God is holy, we are. Because He gave us a living soul, we know Him, the Living God.

The Crucified Lord God, the Risen Lord we belong to.

Abiding

In the course of my years, I look at thinking through a god lens since my baptism of the Holy Spirit—my third baptism.

My prayers over this community are usually specific.

The day is an excerpt of my well-being. The misery gets caught up in the folds of each day. When there is a pause on a change in the focus, there is a fold. Then comes a continuity of faith.

And life proceeds from faith. From immersion three times comes the new hope, live in love.

To the best of us come moments to pause for pappy to redirect our goings-on.

To worry is human weakness, surrender to His abiding.

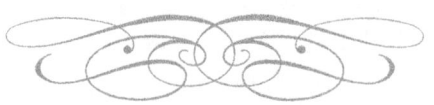

Because You Care

Your presence is all over my life. Kingdom likely. Born of your Spirit. What joy it is to know You.

You saved me from the getup to go. Everything has begun since You came. You have answered all my questions. That is how I wait.

The Lord balances us in our faith to Him. If need be for more attention, He will provide. If we need sorting of our number ones, He will cause conscious choosing.

My conscious choice is Jesus Christ, God Almighty through the Holy Spirit.

Contrasting Communions

Creative skill, inspired graces are God's domain.
Art and Abba.
Wisdom from on High and impulse living.
The domain of graces and morality.
Gifting/rationalized grace/enlightened God/man.
Related people with evidence for supreme closure.
Unity/singular art of many/oneness art reconciled enlightenment truth and justice.
God in Spirit/good.

Awesome

Although I only superficially have known the magisterium, it is in the firmament of my heart. It is the abundant life.

Wonderful love is Jesus. In song, we see Him; the Holy Spirit, speaking through us.

To the few, signs and wonder occurred to bring humility. And death became a gateway to God.

My thought is of apostacy. How easy it is to change God's message. Once truth is mitigated, it becomes ours, truth.

To distill my thoughts and feelings, God has touched me. Now I am led to keep with Him. It may not only be Him alone I keep with, but also His Kingdom.

A Perfect Fit

One left with some feeling after all ends its consuming grace, is one left with some graces unbounded. Unbounded merit is grace spoiling on one's person.

This suffrage of withdrawal must find the cross of life. As though abandoned in thoughtfulness. A necessary closure for the healer. The power of his name carries faith. The unregarded hurt in the other and the command for viciousness she has garnered by self-destructive thinking she has in closure. Unlike that, in tested shallow waters for myself.

Closure needs peaceful thinking, beyond ours. Faith.

A Final Kiss

Death cannot hold one. We live forever. The visceral leaves a mark for God. If one is drawn to Him, all is majestically healed with His new life and Church body.

Worship heals us that way. And the visceral is where God is alive for us.

In God, we see the victory of His hand on everyone.

In my case, I could make love to a woman and she could be satisfied, although she was neutered, and I remained clear as all on my past was canceled.

The truth of the matter is that nothing happened but a completion on our parts, not a consummation as intercourse.

A Living Soul Is Jesus

We all have a Christ figure made within. Is it with some greater capacity in the figuring of Jesus or Abba? What does the Holy Spirit figure indeed, Yesha or Yawheh? What is the figuring of the Holy Spirit within us? A resurrected son or Jehovahs. He is the completion of the law and prophets. Not merely the laws but love for all. That is the completion of the law. The prophets merely spell out the law in love. It takes a human soul totally given to God to say what He means for human souls not so given totally over to God.

Agape, for the Love of God

It is God's unconditional love I write, the force behind everything. The force of God that changed me into a believer (John 3:16).

I have written two volumes worth of articles on just that love, awesome.

Writing lets me take a third person narrative.

The people here are genuine and authentic. God blesses my neighbors.

In Christ,
Peter

<u>Attn</u>:

I am a fool for the way Christ leads me. I am a fool to think I know better.

My hope is that we will reconcile and not argue.

And Jesus

What we want to know is if we are on solid grounding with our faith.

It begins at home, then the holy family and ends with the Holy Trinity.

It ends with us honoring over the weaknesses of our neighbor.

The way of life is my own mystery. His life intercedes constantly by relationship of His Church and mine. Faith couples with faith. My surrender and His ambitions.

Where His life and mine intersect is at the midpoint of His will for me.

It is all fate for me and Jesus.

A Holy Spirit Man

They have come for Him. Their flesh is quiet. They are inquisitive. They take well the peace of the moment. When they are ready, they follow the spirit.

In due time, their flesh is enraptured by the Spirit, and a balance is struck between what was Spirit and flesh and now is believer and Jesus Christ, relationship by the Helper.

That is where I am now.

One with God, the holy family and mankind and myself.

It is all by the Comforter.

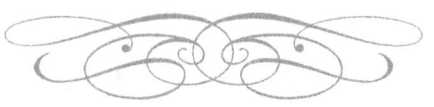

Amen

The Master calls us homeward. The kingdom of God has its seal on us, church. We have been baptized. He finds us in His graces.

He renders new graces through us. New life means new closure of the past and new frontiers present in further matured "Christocentricities."

We become grace-led kingdom residents. The kingdom of God goes with us.

We become ambassadors.

Gracious ways shine graces.

We are exempt from inequity. Sinners, we remain repentant. Abba is gracious.

We all are kin. He knows. Jesus is alive, and we are blessed by the power of God.

Challenges for Our Souls

We say hello to each other. The saints live through us. And reconciliation is made. God is present. His Spirit is alive. My mom is alive as is my whole family in spirit for me and all.

And all in spirit have forgiveness through Jesus.

The life we carry is Him, our true being in spirit life. Spirit life we have passed through the event of baptism with peace for our Lord and heaven for His saints. In truth, it is His kingdom we are in; the kingdom of God for Almighty is our reconcilement.

When time goes forward, God has greater callings on our souls.

Yahweh: Deliverer

We are His children and of His spiritual kingdom, the church of Jesus. We come into knowledge of HS gifts and are gifted with charismata of the Holy Spirit. We are of His church. We seek the Father's.

He is the church most holy and right. We are pilgrims to it by will.

Our task is to be heaven sent for His worship and prayer. We are adopted so.

We are named by His Word. Our life is a nomad in the desert.

Our life is toward all virtue to abound in our time with God the Father.

Christ, the Selfless One

Disciples never mature greater than their Master (Acts 11:26).
Evil wants to have mastering

The one who reverses the roles is the Antichrist. For him, the law is his defense. Grace is a hollow blessing. He is the blessing. His active time was caught off for selfish reasons. He never was a seeker. He presumed to be the "raison d'être." He wanted to be filled, not emptied of his spirit. The Church was a threat, not a means of emptying for the new wine. I could see some leading over their brand of religion, instead of seeing the Church as an icon for emptying their religiosity. The past soul wants the Gospel.

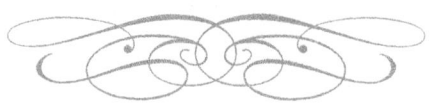

Abba Papa

The strength we have is to serve God. We are a prayer of His to the Father, inspired. The running of His way with us sets our character. The way is alive. It runs within us. It is salvation. It is the movement of the Holy Spirit. The movement of the Holy Spirit is worship music to God.

We sing through the movement of God in us. The Holy Spirit aligns us with the prayers of God.

Praise God that He looks so deeply within our relation with Him.

Companionships

The fortune of heaven lies with its grace of the Trinity. It is a fortitude invulnerable, the source of all grace for Creation. Beauty and aged wisdom form a youth of being. Salvation for all.

The source of being is holy. Faith in God moves His holiness. We are touched as well.

We find Him and come to Him through salvation. It is all gifted, His grace. It's all God.

This becomes our life, children of the kingdom. This is our youth, to answer Holy God in faith. We grow in faith as we grow closer to Him in abiding graces.

The final step of holiness is to grow into godliness.

Coming Together

Love matches the soul. The overarching ache of the soul is to match the void of one with a loving disposition.

The first invitation of this match is inspired.

The way to bring Him in truth to a couple is to linger in the company of each other.

Each conveys a love-in-truth message with the warmth of His love for each.

Being One in Love

Being one is not a simple trick. It takes grace. Inspiration counts heavily. Hearing the Word of God by heart recall helps.

Love as I have loved you.

Be perfect as your Father in heaven is.

God is love.

The Holy Spirit will help. The rescue will come in the ordinary day's events, seeing God is in control.

The power of His name carries all to fulfillment.

Being one is not a solitary confinement but a one-on-one relationship with God and my neighbor each separately.

A Call for Life

In being Christian, we need to answer the Holy Spirit. It means not always being involved in some call but growth. Acknowledging His words as source material, but that time may be undesirable is an option. It means there is empowering capacitation meant for us. We may need to translate His message across our needs.

Being Christian means being full of Him so one's faith gifts Him.

It is a hunger of no limit to affect His will.

When we are, He is so real so that life is before us by what worship we are through Him.

A Christian is blind to his self and open to His.

Only the reward of love can match the efforts of God to place His good. We are immersed in Him so that His love takes place.

He wants to reward us, blessing us beyond creativity to His very essence.

His mystery puts us on a sacred source with Him as our salvation develops. It is here. He is so we have, being of Him.

Being with His Stillness

In between our moments, God causes our life to be with Him. He separates our nature in those moments as godly or ungodly. It is a sign of our surrender to Him.

In our walk come moments of quiet despair when we find ourselves in a process of relinquishing to His surrender something that speaks as a loss or emptying of what we would call reality for His reality.

At these times, the life we give over to Him seems a match for the life we gain in His reality.

Ultimately, we may be a part of His great stillness, where pervading holiness holds our wills together. Such a oneness frees us to act in His conscience. We are set free to Him in all manner of circumstance, in actuality and faith. Now reason discerns the logic of faith.

It means our prayers walk in the very life we are in His life, and that they come true by how we set Him free into reality.

By how we submit. He finds honor in us.

Coming to Him

Living is finding a cure for messes and an answer to death. Living presents us full of opinions and beliefs.

It is here faith enters. Here, God is a symbol of life's faith. He is its fruition.

The Lord places His trust in us so we can complete each day. His way is to bring forth truth in our life so we can measure how He lies in us.

We want to be His, and this can only be if truly we lie within His interior.

When we think of the Lord, He amazes us with His sovereignty.

He brings us to a reality in Him that makes all His answer.

When He brings us within His fold, He cares so we are strong with anointing and grace. He wants us to extend His hand.

He hopes His mystery through us as mystic knowledge of life.

The times we enjoy with His life are the transformations of our spirit.

A Vision for Life

When time travels, we are beckoned to follow. Eternity calls to us but is not so readily seen.

When time enters our life, we give special notice of what is at stake. In eternity, our focus is on the Lord. We drift between both visions.

As we walk into His life, a convergence takes place. We see God in all circumstances as we continue to trust in Him.

The value of our vision is in what we give an indication of life's reality. Whether we see one perspective or another is not so vital as to how fully we engage in that life. God views us through the fullness of His life. How the two meld is His mystery for us. That is our walk of faith.

The fullness of our life is a result of which spiritual virtue comes into play for most of our life. That is the fullness God looks upon us through. When we look in this life, we know God.

Being Christ-Like

Life with God is an enchanting pleasure. He reaches deep and finds us inside. We are illuminated by His tenderness. His nature is to bring togetherness. He does this with the promptings of His Spirit.

As we make our faith upon His walk, we are blessed to see Him reveal good in each of us. Having righteousness is something we can only suggest how loving He is.

We make our walk the dayspring of faith from us. To know God is to find how love intersects and manifests with us.

The kindred nature of the Spirit reveals us to be created so His delight can be our salvation. Each time we enter in, our faith is a stepping stone for sanctification. To be so blessed is to have clarity and vision. It all takes this for us to see that we are God's revelation, His image.

Being One

When we discern what life is, it all comes from His essence. It is love. Any discernment that shows the believer's heart and not God's is false.

Judgment is not to shelter bias but to bring people into a real love. It is not to kill them with attachments but rather to free them of them.

There was a time before the Holy Spirit made God indwelling. Then justice was based on a legal covenant and not an indwelling one.

Thus, this age of grace requires us to apply a grace with love when we act through our convictions.

This is the deepening of the process of His life, to draw us closer so we can together be His Church and not scattered.

The devil will have no part in us finding His love. All of us are His love. Separate, we will not grace glory.

Coming Home

When Jesus comes to us, we are removed of hindering attachments. Our soul is freed to Him.

The more this happens, the softer our heart becomes. So soft that the Holy Spirit convicts our very being of having faith in Jesus. So assured we are elders of His faith, seeing well where unity draws all His people into His fullness.

Sometimes, even elders cannot distinguish faith from superstition, so remarkably interwoven they are. As good and evil are in this life. We cannot destroy what is of faith to get at what holds superstition. We must allow Christ to make an end-time harvest of this wheat so we don't prematurely pull out the weeds.

Even elders need to divest themselves of their raiment of faith and enter the experience of others with simply a heart of faith. And witness how differently they carry their cross. Then one can remark on the wonderful unity in His Church.

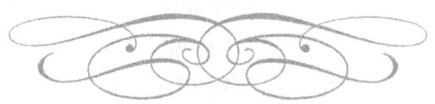

Covenant Trust

The way of fiscal health is to trust the Lord.

He is in covenant with us. We love Him. He has faith in us as kingdom children.

Our love is a trusting love. His faith is agape love.

Hope is all and vital. It must be. To be without it is to be without being.

To trust the Lord takes the Holy Spirit in one's life. He must master one and Jesus be God. Then one can trust the Father.

Before Him

Glory to God in the highest for His control of the heart strings. Put your mind on higher things to coax the heart. If you are a changed or saved person, then the Holy Spirit will help. Otherwise, you are to have another encounter, transubstantiation of faith, the Holy Spirit deposit or change to revealing Him. You are being groomed for relationship.

He has chosen you and will not stop until you have a complete change for Jesus Christ.

Then and further will be your gifting/special way you are before God. Then you can praise Him for your overcoming.

A Kiss

We need a buddy to track our inner thoughts. These feelings are primary to how we interpret life or even have a grasp of life, where it begins and how it goes forth.

Discernment keys through all of their mystery. Truth runs right through all of this.

As beginning goes, truth unveils itself. We spent our time futilely until we see the inspiration of the Holy Spirit.

Called

The view that takes all into account is enlightened. Like the constitution or such documents, the Word speaks through them. We are transliteral people by the Gospel message. Our spoken names make us transliteral beings in anointed prayer. We cross over from one entity to another in Christ. We are charged with graces for one life to another life in Jesus Christ.

To be anointed one must have the silent Gospel in mind and heart for a candidate. The Holy Spirit comes forth by the Gospel. Prayers like this with an utterance naming the candidate make for the anointing framework.

Christening Life

So stupid are the errors we make. A trap by Him has no good choice. We can only check to see if we abide well with His power of love.

Sometimes, we are not to make a decision but be close to God. It is a time for humility and growth.

For all sold-out believers, God is always waiting and testing our faith. With patience, we can overcome the adversary's positions. All it takes is sure faith in God and abiding graces. Just continue all empowered ways.

Love Him before loving any gift. We are a transported to the christening of life to life.

Coming Together as a Part of His Glory

All comes together at His control. Death no longer limits mankind. We are freed to life.

Resurrection is the wonder of God, to live beyond and to overcome limits.

We are that overcoming people now heralding God.

We are Spirit-led born-again disciples of Jesus Christ. We carry a gospel, framed by the Gospel of God, salvation.

We are freed of life without Him. The kingdom of God is present to all His.

Abba

Beauty and wisdom are Jesus Christ. Just as grace and truth are. What in each of us is a lack is beauty and grace. It is a law of ourselves. Each time in God is Christ, until there is Christ to us each. The encounter of the love of God is our talesman. A faith to God from each, only through His encounter. That is our gospel. We take out of the love of God anointed. There is imperfect surrender. The Holy Spirit aids us there.

Yes, daddy dear daddy. You are the closest to Jesus and Mary's Holy Father!

A New Change! Overcome

The wallbuilders.com is one source that has led me to my "All for America" approach (Rom. 8:28).

Civil disobedience is a greatly overlooked power of our politics.

It's like our Christian religion. Abortion has been greatly overlooked.

The institution of the Church has been greatly overlooked as a source of faithfulness and hope.

All these are American icons that have failed. We need a fresh charge in this country, faithful to God and His graces, us.

Look at the framers of the constitution. They were facing terrible odds and they overcome them.

Crisis Is Reality without Healing

What does it mean to give Him your heart and soul? It means to give Jesus' name appropriate over to Him based on our rendering of faith. How we trust in Him is a measure of faith. When we reach crisis, trust can be absolute. How we maintain faith is recognizing the need for some perpetual trust. And this is done by prayer, sitting for the atmosphere for faith to exist and form a trust in God. What we call the reality of the times constitutes the nature of atmosphere our prayers live in.

Can We Agree

Coming into accountability is us at a crisis. Using such as a view, we can see levels, eased and strict. Freedoms are acknowledged graces. What they are and when they occur is important. Why they occur is in view of our innocence. What it provides for us is bonding and trust. Should it be work that set the standard?

It all reflects a sobriety of mind and a well-composed spirit.

How faith agrees or not with law is a learning we may not get. It means for setbacks and overcoming, with grace, to get over them to a quiet with Jesus.

The soul needs quiet rebuilding.

Broken and Afflicted

When we overcome, the miracle happens; we see and believe.

I can believe in the truth of things with His touch.

Then I have discernment. The Truth, Life, and Way are Jesus Christ. We resurrect with Him. Look to His life in you and in the Church. Theme, there is a meeting to answer your faith in Jesus.

His presence.

What a joy when He reveals Himself. We are in Him for no small reason; the living of the Gospel for the afflicted.

At Peace or Broken

For one not to see inspiration in my writings is to see plainly, not discernably. One too in touch with the ways of the Church in out of touch with the Holy Spirit.

Holy Spirit writings take well to one broken for Jesus, not simply the godsend.

To be broken for Christ, one must face Him with a bottomless crisis.

Facing God, one finds wholeness from the cross.

Berean Interpretation

A thoughtful quest is encouraged, as all are well considered.

God enters and all has salt on it. He makes whole the quiet to the heart.

Blessings resound in the quiet; healings are profuse and profound.

The different writing styles make for different conglomerations of spiritual aptitudes and notations.

Stylistic different views of cursive and printed versions are conscious notes of care and importance.

Ultimately, there is no difference.

Attack or Advance

The top forward area of the brain seems in contact with prayer life.

The very nature of gifting is set by one's walk. Inspiration follows the constant path of obedience or affliction. It is healing or magnifying of His grace.

One can request specific grace to come. If one encounters shame, blame, guilt, or comparison, then back off to see if it is a test of the Lord or trap of the devil.

The way is edifying and simple. Otherwise, it's a trap and to be avoided for forth deeper in God.

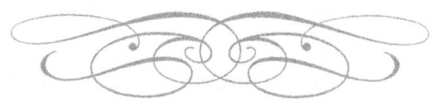

A Newness of Spirit

In our kingdom walk, we are preparing to walk fully with Him. Salvation, trusting. Worship always takes heart, to swell with faith.

Our discernment of truth yields us to kingdom life.

We see His kingship over our lives and that we are friends, meaning we take Him very seriously. We are disposed to view things on their spiritual basis.

Our hearts are circumcised, meaning we take His words right into our very being. A new spirit is being derived by the work of our faith and the Holy Spirit. The tribulations we experience is the offering of our heart, soul, and spirit to Him when He resurrects off the body.

A Kingdom Walk

The Paschal mystery of Christ all Christians are caught up in. This is the role of salvation, to bring us through the passion to His glorification, the creation of His kingdom.

As we face victory in life with Jesus, we look to the abundant life with Him, a kingdom walk. The Paschal mystery gathers all our faith in God. It is our means to His end. This way is holiness before Him. The abundant life means to put us right with His Paschal mystery so we are in victory with Him. It comes down to following the Church life of Jesus, making each day another victory.

Celebrate

We ask only to be where He wants.
He is open to us finding Him. Love is the option.
We love because He is near.
We are Holy Spirit children of the kingdom when we know Him. To know Him is to love Him.
God is near because we love Him. We are part of His kingdom. It goes wherever we go. And He is a big part of it.
All the power of Christ is upon us by the Holy Spirit. Our God is a Living God. And all who have faith in Him have life with His Son, Jesus Christ.
We sip off His blood every time we celebrate His kingdom and rule.

At the Core Joy

The joy of the Lord in the beauty He bestows for us in this life, a forerunner to heaven. Certainly not a replacement. Too much beauty is ascribed to have and not in the hereafter.
Our aging of our youth dictates much of how our learning will proceed.
The joy of the Lord we are to follow for our healing beauty, Jesus Christ is to be seen in all.
Our time spent on earth is to learn afflicted life. At the core of darkened ways is light. The life we lead is darkened light.
God's plan is John 3:16. We are no longer of the dark but of the light.

Broken Always

Heartened we are in Christ, knowing grace. That profundity, grace. It exemplifies holy and personal God. Just is our behavior toward Him.

The glory of God is his grace. This grace translates to our personalization of faith to God and to our neighbor. He personalizes faith for us.

It is the power of the cross unto salvation.

He, Jesus, is all wonderment. The Messiah is as beyond description as is the power of God, Jehovah-Yahweh. He has personalized Himself to Father, Son, and Holy Spirit. Just humility seeks Him, to ever abide.

Co-Inheritors

For the godly, Jesus has overcome the world, defeated the devil and helps us crucify the Flesh on the altar of heaven.

The broken sold out to Christ find shelter under the fellowship of His Catholicism.

We are broken to allows us to have total surrender of our will for His.

In all our doings is the unity of the Holy Spirit. He masters us to Christ Almighty. There we are inheritors of the Father's grace.

A Call for Holiness

The presence of God, reflected in whole manners and thoughts, graces the lifestyles of believers. It is a carryover of abundant life issues.

These realities make imminent the good, God Almighty.

These are all part of victorious living, the grace-led living of positivism, Jesus Christ.

The holy walk imitating the Gospel is a transformed Spirit giftedness.

"Seek first his kingdom and his righteousness" (Matt. 6:33).

Focusing on the Holy Giver ignites these pathways.

By Fields of Grace

We watch as grace changes all we know. By fields of grace flooding us, we become spiritual.

We gain insight over revelation. Fellowship yields good fruit.

The kind words used for describing the way we go to Him embolden us past sins of all types. We realize what a tight fellowship we have.

Love is a sacred art we see in many ways. What God shares with us is indescribable. Our home is with the Lord, our heaven.

An Incarnation of Hope

God is the architect of our lives. We cannot say what we have encountered that He has made provision for us. Certainly more than we can imagine. It's tied up in faith.

He leaves us with the mind of our "Christliness" and the power of His Spirit. There is stigma on all levels for us to deal with. Stigma takes our human and divine strengths.

There is no lane where God operates and we don't. He knows of our ability and lack of it. He has decided what ability we have, so we have authority over stigma like He does.

We work in concert directing a symphony that makes music of our relationship.

We are in a battle against chaos—chaos on the divine front and on the human one. Jesus is the light of this incarnation.

Beyond His Presence

The first resolution a Holy Spirit person must make is the constant presence of God.

The inspiration is there. It must be freed of catch places.

The threshold of grace is the altar of heaven. In Jesus's name we offer peace in our prayers. Death is refashioned to hold grace for life.

It is on the way of filled graces, to empty our human ways for godly one. Some may have passed to those graces and still be here. Only a Christly soul can cross this divide.

A Loving God

It has taken several changes, encounters, to be with the Lord.

Each time, some circumstance or person has relationally affected me toward Him.

The love of the Lord is the central theme of the heart. How we play with the Maker suits our companionship with Him or even our ego with Him.

Our graces need tending and that means for us to keep loving contact with Him and fellowship.

We need to keep grace at our forefront and not the end of power or influence, God's work.

Developing Our Mystery of Christ

Life proceeds then departs. That is the nature of life. To be so nonconformist is to be only true to our mind. To not let the heart breathe with faith is not to see eternity's grip on our life. We are in a mystery that develops with worship for Christ.

It means love is and we are because God did not give us life in vain. He brought this gift so we could share in fellowship.

We are torn between the attachments of this life and the healing of us. It is a healing which takes us past life into eternity. It means we must be conscious of the nature of sin upon our lives and of how faith generates.

Our walk invites our sensitivity. In its function, we entertain reality by the Spirit in our choosing of how He will function with our will. We all have our depth of faith in which our sensitivity is highlighted. That is who Christ is to us.

Insight

We look at ourselves and wonder. What is insight if it does not capture the wonder of it all!

Insight means noticing something no more as it has been but at a stage beyond where you used to be with it. It means seeing the opening of the door of revelation to show something fuller of life.

It means we pass to new paradigms and see other ones in a newly different light.

Insight means just that sight from within. Getting there is a fest of mountains and valleys.

If we just look at the scoring of activity upon each hill and valley, we will see a message of insight for the totality we are. The traits of life reveal who we are.

What we need to tap into is how God is with us so much so He and we are one.

Being So Christlike

Once we come into God with fullness, there is nothing that does not hold a presence of Him within.

It's seeing with the eyes of faith the love He has made all to live in. We are then a new Adam for we can see the good of God in all in spite of the apparent evil in all.

It was when man fell from grace that evil and good formed the nature of life. Only the redeemed man can see the good all the time in all. The less than redeemed see only or generally an evil in the world. Even if we only partially see evil, we have not arrived. The godly walk on a higher ground.

Jesus calls each of us to be godly and live so. The pursuit of this is where we all are. Some may look godly yet that is what looks. The faithful seek God because they have not a completely godly being and life. They have not arrived into full Christliness.

His Prayer

What we call love consists of a delegating priory suited to our satisfaction. What we need is to be imbued with a sense of worship to reach His inspiration and make our dead love come alive. Love can only have breath to live if it is free unconditionally.

And what was once a priory becomes displaced in His will.

It is our life as His prayer that makes this all possible. There is His will.

My love in God exists. I know because His is in me. He sets free the stony heart. He makes it give forth the warmth of flesh. Love is imbued with His inspiration.

In faith, we know Him with what changes our life, love. When we love, we give life to what lies in our interior. It comes to wisdom. We discover a vision for us.

The mystery of life is completed with love. We are just beginning.

Who Am I?

When we come into spirituality, we are broken and lost. The net result is to find healing and Christ.

Anxiety appears when we feel emotionally broken. It's a natural warning signal that can be aggravated by the simple stress in dwelling. Being lost is an identity problem which Christ solves. Being emotionally broken requires steady healing. Distortions of thought can take place because of it.

We are made of love, and sin has exploited us. Christ sets us free. He decided our love would be healed by His so it is whole.

I am diseased by life, raised to newness by His life. It all takes time for redemption to be complete, eternity. Then our faith in God is no longer a question but a certain justice.

As we move to God and find healing, every day Jesus brings us closer to His life and further from the problems of this life.

Faith

Giving God His due is the goal of our life. To serve and be complete within.

He guides us to truth pertinent to our life so He can lead us into His life by giving over those burdens. In this way, He makes service a thing of revelation.

Being complete within means accepting Him in the fullness He is to us.

In this manner, we come into fullness of Him and are brought to spiritual health in Him.

The spiritual walk one takes is full of attachments and detachments. We need to clearly address what Christ desires in both cases. That is our spiritual heath. Certainly, we want to be so very well to honor and receive His fullness.

The Lord asks us into Him. How can we unless the fullness we receive of Him is coupled to the fullness of us. The selflessness of us is dependent on this relation by our check and balance of detachments.

This is the course of strengthening faith.

Light

The light shines and transfigures us. We are transparent conceived all of His Spirit.

Our ableness to cast love is a reflection of our transparency.

Transfiguration is transcending glory falling on us. The light is the instrument of the Lord. We become the light through Christ.

Light shines upon my soul, and I am renewed. The light is the love of fellowship.

Fellowship is how God lets the soul worship. It is mystic relationship. Legacy is the summation of this.

What we offer is a light for the Lord to bear us into truth. It is a holy discernment that lets Christ reign upon us. He is the gift of light.

Finding God in Our Midst

There lies a fate we all face death. More terrible than that is the fate of the godless.

They are trapped by their hindsight. Without redemption, they just enter the void after life.

God represents their ability to be freed and of loving character. Yet they have resisted any effort for Him to find their heart at flesh.

We need to see how limited they are, irreproachable. They cannot contain many relationships. They are overcome and need to let go of relationships when the risk at stake becomes sensitive. They need basic functions unimpeded by comment.

There is a middle ground where one is not threatened, and we have opportunity for relationship.

It means coming off your high horse and being more Christlike. Relationships form by respected bounds.

Entering Eternity

In the most deceiving manner, the devil returns us to our basis humility. Our human self returns as we are reacquainted with our "old man."

It is a familiar rut. Learning to deny ourselves and detach our soul from ourselves is the difficulty of becoming selfless. But it is necessary to become His person by faith that images His soul upon us.

As we develop courage in Him, we learn to put our attention beyond mere soulful demands to actualizing our faith in Him into selfless expressions of compassion and unconditional loving. Here our discernment is key in giving us this access.

One's relationship becomes more like teamwork as one learns maturity by His example in the mystical marriage. The will seeks oneness, and the soul is pregnant with His direction. Thus, we occupy Him in spirit.

But it all comes down to a conscious agreement of His victory for our life.

Prayer

The opening of the heart to the passage of faith is prayer.

Our surrender to His sovereignty is our key. Submission.

The light is the presence of prayer, what draws the supernatural and natural together.

The gift of faith passes in prayer to bring harmony in this life and His.

The value of prayers is in the transforming of the heart to one's salvation walk.

The Lord values His will in bringing about answer to prayer. It is a sign of His higher call that we surrender to. He does remedy each prayer we bring. He only requires the Spirit be free in us. He deserves a special honor of us, broken and contrite.

His Church is where hearts unite under His prayer for them.

Mulling

In the furrows of my mind lay hidden several terse and problematic thoughts. Reconciliation is not so clear as well as their exact nature. They seem to speak of incidents not get full in their comprehension, as if one were in a dream. And waking up meant reality.

I only want to make a proper response. But things seem only to escalate.

I am very tired of the consummate wisdom we need and only hope for a simple focus.

Relations are enigmatic and leave us with pieces. I am only too certain what has been a growing experience has not found the end.

In the end, I can see all of life clearing. Now there is only a blur.

In anticipation of the peace that transcends, I give away my worries freely. And ask for Him to come to me.

Here in devotion I find Him and my satisfaction.

To be so detached that life is real in me.

Unfolding Eternity

What God asks is if we are truly alive for Him. Whether God is the essence of our life, or whether we are. Then He wants to shine to transform us as light so we can be a prophetic revelation of Jesus.

To be His, an eternal word, is to see as eternity unfolds upon the time of this life. He asks us to hasten and make known the passage of His life over this one.

The mortality of this life disappoints us. But His life is faith to becoming eternal.

It is faith that nurtures and the chaos of mortality that robs. The devil knows this because he wishes to veil us and keep us. God does not want to keep us but emancipate us into His glory. One way points to our limits, another to His greatness.

To be His eternal word of life means knowing what He has for us. A faith to nurture is what He gives to us. It is the unfolding of revelation upon our life.

Glorify God, Pray

Prayer is our attempt to come closer to the grace necessary of spirit to pass us deeper into His love for us and for others.

It is not a material quest but a humane quest. And that is how He answers.

Prayer forms especially to the needs involved.

The denomination of the church bears into the ideas of inclusion and exclusion. These ideas require acceptance and no mitigation. This is "gospel" for the faith of the individual.

Faith is described by prayer.

Lack of faith is expressed by lack of prayer. When we determine faith is the expression of love for Christ, then prayer becomes that expression.

Ritual is when prayer lacks the expression of faith. The inspiration of God is missing. Instead, it is an act to satisfy our humanity.

Alive with God

The steps of the kingdom are leaps of faith.

The regard we have of ourselves is repentant sinners, for He is all of God and all man.

We fail to recognize the steps of faith when we see Him through natural eyes. We need to see the supernatural way upon the divine to see Him and accept Him in our life of living.

We need Holy discernment from the Holy Spirit.

Can we positively answer the question, "Is the HS actively in our life?" Are we emphatically celebrating Jesus's life in our life every day or not?

Bring Jesus to life and carry yourself into life with Him.

Icon of Living Selflessness

We are meant to find our finish in Him. The free will is the truth, life, and way, once transformation takes hold. The HS then masters us for destiny in Christ. We identify Jesus as the Messiah, and we are in passion with His lie on the cross. Our cross matches the offering Jesus made of selflessness to the Father. The free will is our nature to hold onto Jesus, blind faith. We are assumed into His glory, His life and way. It is the kingdom leap of faith, beyond the ordeal of change. We are a Christ child of God.

Love makes many turns in us with His raising from the grave.

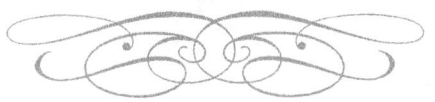

Faith that Carries Our Cross

The energy to turn to faith comes from a tragic hero.

Something has to end for a life change, Jesus. A divine life is more potent than a natural disruption by any means. And a supernatural divine power of life is the only thing that can restore all to their good state.

Are we really saying that Jesus the Son of God is the only and real Messiah of all? He is the peace of God.

We worship God through Jesus's walk of life.

Good, honest worship revives His oneness and puts faith alive.

The Constitution of Christ, Revelation

The epitome of change is the constitution. Gathered in age to age, it seeks to make conformance.

Jesus is the One completed in the words of the Holy Spirit. That is, it's constitution. His very living.

The minor elements of population render a spice to the majority. However deemed, the majority is subject to the minorities input. In the USA, the revelations of the minors bring revolution to the major element (White, European). It is a synthesis of truth, Jesus.

Another Constitution Healed

Holy healer is God. He takes the dirt and makes it handsome, graced.

Indeed, the revelations of the Lord are many. He is a serving Lord.

The handsome One. He is tuned to the heart.

There are many persuasions.

It rises from element to life. He is in focus of Him.

Many seek with no return. Revolution is handled by constitution. Alive and altogether different, as one all.

Grace, Not Bias

The way of the Spirit is to hearten our vision. The vision is of grace, and it is ever expanding. It is us and our reality that grows with the heartbeat of the Holy Spirit. He is a healing Spirit of power and truth. We accept Him and a refreshment of our past, to the renewal of our mind.

The motive of the HS is to perfect, make holy, our giftedness from Him, to encourage the range of our fellowship with Him.

The range of our fellowship is a way we transfer the light of His grace.

The means of politics is to honor what is good and lasting as a constitutional land.

The Path

Where we go with faith in everywhere, seeking an impossible host with God. Little patience reveals poor judgment. We will always be different. Because now we have entered a spiritual life. It is a shared entity of God. All of God or little of us. We are all within all. To each, we enter their enclave with the all of God and our All. Rest is God's all for you.

Thank You, Jesus. Praise God Almighty for the deft inspiration of the Holy Spirit, creating a fork where none existed, pure faith. Thank You, Lord.

Be of light, true and honest. Love your God with others of faith.

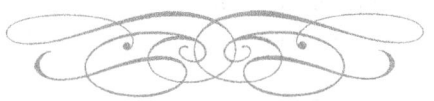

A Simple Course of Social Grace

Our country was built on revelation. The basis for change is constitutional. The model is the Son of God. Total grace made to fit a society and all its quirts. This requires handling a people that may not be grace observant, boundaries to preserve freedom. God is here, so we preserve a spirit of holiness to arbitrate all matters. Since this higher source may get lost, have one instituted to maintain this spirit. Consequences may lack in overall graciousness. This happens when laws defy the very freedoms they protect.

The Country of Heart

Jesus is the model. Love with a passion for people. People need to have other mindfulness.

The different nature of Jesus Christ should show how difficult it is for people to be totally selfless in love.

Without revelation, the work of God is impossible.

All tied together the private time of representatives is important.

The constitution of Jesus is the sum of revelation of the Bible. The sum of human experience lies with prayer to Jesus. The work of Jesus is music.

Us and God Alone

Rhema is the personal use of the ordinate word, Jesus Christ. Visions of Him are according to the tenderest prayer of Him in the most explicit manner of Him to us.

The qualifications of any one of the Trinity are at the core of our tenderest prayers or movements of faith. God is smiling and calling us to deepen salvation.

The Book of Life is written in our heart, Jesus and mine. The atmosphere is Jesus. It is the Holy Spirit and the Father calling us to deepen faith.

The Indisputable

We may tender such a spirit of acceptance we physically, not just spiritually, know of Him. After all, God and His heavenly host are divinely supernatural. And we can register such in this state of acceptance.

What we may see is through holy discernment. We may, at first, call it imagination. But it is a gift, we wholly given to Jesus Christ. Our physical abilities register it.

The more we discern the Word, the more our discerning crosses over to the kingdom.

He rewards the seeker. We may in time have our fill of His convincing and decide all in His times. However for the seeker goes, he has all the answers.

The Cup of Power Meant to Be

Who do we know but God and His family? We are and so are the perks we inherit. We are sealed into their presence. At them, we are a discovery well reckoned with.

Make no mistake; we have been looked at our whole life long by the magisterium. At all our milestones of faith, we have been kept with the holy graces. At times, the outpouring of grace was monumental. Never to be forgotten in "rhematenic" far beyond the Word's ordinate one.

The personal word to us over life is where the Lord speaks of His life, where He is speaking to us, is power.

Radiant of Graces

We are repentant sinners. All the time confessing. Until we are sealed in His faith and Spirit, Jesus Christ. All grace.

A true believer is one with Christ. One of the spiritual Church.

One sees beyond any anger in God, through His Holiness, to His pure spirit of faithfulness.

The ultimate kingdom journey happens when we give up this life. For the meantime, we can be comforted by God's supernatural presence which is guided with us by His Spirit, the Holy Spirit. Such inspiration is a manifestation of our reality.

Holy Theology

Strongholds must be broken, and high places must be brought down.

Karma, luck, and demonic influence.

We are driven by grace. And no substitute for it. We are only interested in true movements of the heart, charismata, grace-led idealisms. To be in grace is to be in the kingdom. We are not pure spirit, but the Holy Spirit is. And in heart, we receive Jesus Christ. Through the Holy Spirit with the prayers of Mary. We conceptualize in Jesus and the holy host.

Packaged for Paradise

We spend untold hours in quiet here. We wait for His Word to take us into His immortal paradise.

How close He has been over these years. Kind of heart and always to our prayers.

He has kept me surely on our road with Him. Jesus has been our defender and hope.

Sometimes, we now murmur over things but ultimately are reassured of His presence with us.

His grace perfects us perfectly. We only need look at Him, and all is restored. He keeps us in everlasting grace.

God Decides on His Touch

He is near and far with His oneness. He abides within His presence and person. That He can go from one to the other decides. He is almighty. It's all in the winds of the HS. Emmanuel is always with us, as is the presence of God. He can at any time substantiate His forms. He is God, here, within and beyond, all in the time of now. Brotherhood never felt so good.

Although He has conquered the world, we still have to be careful of flesh dominance, but we have to avoid risk.

All God Is for, Abba

My dad was better than I deserved.

Mom was always a friend.

God was always there. JC and the Holy Spirit became any best pale for life.

All else became my history with God and His people.

I am God blessed and God's.

Abba is daddy. I am a recovered mental patient who knows the people of His kingdom. All are in His kingdom, some struggling more than others.

All Aboard

God is the One. Holy and omnipotent. The holy family are all His creations.

Widows and orphans are the true ones of religion.

We all are.

A small humor carries the land.

We are blessed knowing at least one friend, godly at best.

The wind blows HS. The day is the darker. Lord God rules my heart.

The ocean forgets. We are all His.

My day is short. He comes.

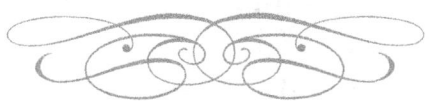

Thank You, God

I look back in time and see how it couldn't have turned out any other way.

I surely didn't deserve the breaks I got. God's mercy. God's in our lives. God entered my will.

A life of grace is the best way to describe my life with God in His kingdom—kingdom steps for me.

I have an understanding. God is number one. With Him, the door is timely opened.

At the time I realize the fact, the answer is given, Jesus.

The door of opportunity opens heater.

It's that simple.

Constant faith.

The Maker's Touch

You are as sweet as one from Camelot. The inner wishes of your Savior guide you.

You have a home here according to your wishes. The company of friends has been carefully screened.

In this company, you are to find peace within and acceptance. It is a small patch of heaven to remind you where your good graces come from—a delivered heart.

Be one among many who are pleasing to the Lord.

It is your welcome to the higher graces of your Maker. Be a soul afraid with Spirit.

Beginnings and Losses

The terrible loss is in a field state, spiritual poverty. The Lord God is able and more. Each takes kingdom steps. Worship heals.

A terrible loss can be turned around by the Gospel of Jesus Christ. Out of a desert, finding springs His love and Holy Spirit. One is new.

One is taught in the Spirit. Peace, justice, and love are the hallmarks of the HS.

For some, the Bible speaks. The charismatic is the golden rule to joy. With loss comes absolute surrender, obedience to godly love.

All are failed creatures in a new life, a step from selfless.

The Kingdom of God

Believing in God says an event has taken place. An intimate encounter between God and His believer has happened. A witness of the Lord's touch, a change has happened. A Christian believer has abiding intimacy with God. He knows he is frail, and God knows him. Because He called him out of the world, God tests and challenges his faithfulness. Each day for the believer is a celebration of the life of Christ.

The dark is no more. The light illumines. God is holy.

Worship Life

Kingdom life takes steps with a healed, broken life. It is a transforming gift nature.

The gathered insight of discernment paves the way for revelation.

So gathered it sees us in heart with Jesus. Only then do we abide with His kingdom. It is living with fullness, with God.

We abide with Him with fullness of graces. Our penance each day is to celebrate Christ worship. It is a life given to Him for Him being the Ultimate.

Kingdom life in God, we are in perpetual fellowship.

Wisdom from Brokenness

Prophecy and tongues become God's means for kingdom life to form with giftedness and healed brokenness. My writing falls under three gamers—Christ and I, Christ of God, and God alone.

Worship to Him and reading becomes prime Jesus Christ is found in youthful extensions of the bind and the radiance. The writing was called prolific and a gift, a dove message of the heart.

We all cling to the cross for pure hearts and souls and spirits. We inherit the finality of Jesus Christ to the answering of our prayers of life.

Kingdom Talents

The motion of the HS graces me constantly. Although the HS operates with each of us uniquely by the fellowship of God, His creative magisterium. Every son and daughter of His grace knows and speaks to Him. All questions of life are answered by Jesus Christ. We are His. He is the spark to our grace, the grasp of our reality, and the existential flesh of ours.

What is a skill amplified by the experience of God's touch? A gift. What was a talent in college is a gift for the kingdom.

Jesus the Christ

You know you are blessed when three times what could be a foul play turns out good. You must thank the Spirit. And worship. It was all meant to discern the good about one. Blessed.

To know you are in the hands of a good God, be blessed.

Even a mess accident forever He comes. Thank You, Jesus.

Jesus is the sole reason for life. Lord God Jesus Christ is all hope in glory.

Where scuttlebutt thrives, Jesus is oblivious. Man is flesh and pride. Christ is lost within God. He is the voice in the afflicted.

The Creative

Jesus is the portion for all of us.

He is in all of us to bear us to life.

The fiction in our unbelief. If our desire is not to believe, then what is truth?

Relative natures hoist unbelief as actual believing, not fiction.

We believe the speed of light is the fastest, making it really just a relative nature.

Creative natures are immediate. Truth. They defy chance. No chance but meant to be, just as they are.

They contain answers to all questions through faith. It is the power of faith in Jesus.

The Loving

Our fuss will is governed through the Holy Spirit, or else it is still in basic covenant to God and not absolutely surrendered.

Listen to the Spirit. He will guide your heart.

It is a goodie worth waiting on.

It means to drive our heart into His presence.

The standing applause is the matching of hearts. The breath turns within. The touch becomes unconscious. He reckons with us. We are loving. And our free will has been ransomed to His pleasure.

That's a Goodie and They All Stood Up

Your pleasure is my heaven. I am here to serve at your pleasure, which is my pleasure.

You have overcome the world and the devil. So by my faith in You, so have I. All that remains is my flesh to be put to the cross by faith, which I do by prayer and worship. I try to govern myself this way.

Every good and perfect gift is from heaven above.

The Father governs me to Himself through His Son and Holy Spirit. All the host of heaven call out for me.

In Uncertain Times

The pressure from the HS is clear. Make good on debt to Jesus. Let the Christ rule the heart. Be involved in His inspiration.

I love to hear your voice. It is as though my inner man speaks of conscience—a conscience that picks up every change in tender voltage.

This tender voltage adds up to a major shock when all things are added up. It tells when all things began to their final point.

The result is forgiveness under the power of the cross, authenticity.

In all corner, I find the Holy Spirit, the spirit of truth, working. God allows it as a test or challenge to believers.

He Is

The love of Jesus Christ is all we need. He is total grace unto the Father and the host of heaven. He is the key the Holy Spirit says is life abundant. Blessed are we because God the Father, God the Son, and the Holy Spirit are One for us.

We are holy blessed because of God. He is Lord of all. The heavenly host are our assurance of salvation.

Make straight the way of the Lord. Only He is perfect and all creation is under Him.

In Him, we know how it is and why.

Contemporary Contemplatives

There is a mystery with Chuck, and his healing is mine with God.

Under special knowledge, trust has been formed for prayer.

His victory is the same with me. He sees the chastity of the HS and the holy priesthood of me in Christ. I share this faithfulness of God with Chuck.

The medical concerns are an ordeal. The answer is the affliction for Christ, the Way, and our politics of concern. We find a gravity in the worship. Music draws the believer into the presence.

Following His Commands

To fire up the conscience, the Lord places commands. He keeps us steady to His will for us, desert or overabundance of faith, to keep an absolute surrender. The balance is our offering to the Lord. We have a need to keep a pure and contrite heart. Worship heals us to Him.

Worship needs to touch the soul and uplift the spirit. Be it entertainment, then let be rightly so godly, God focused.

Allow the shekinah glory to hover in the music and draw one to God. Then the presence of Jesus is like heaven, not merely peace. That just means your spirit is ready.

Saving Grace Is Our Affliction

To follow Him and carry your cross comes by way of a healed believer's passion, the inspiration of the Holy Spirit. It is prayer and worship. That is the cross for our life in the kingdom, our absolute surrender, not holiness. It is coming to the fact our affliction is necessary to find Jesus by and our victory in His overcoming grace to find salvation by. It is the will of God for each of us to find Jesus our Savior, not strongholds. Following Him and carrying our cross is a covenant to God we accept His resurrection for our lives' grace and affliction. We become healed to eternal life in this search. Then we know the Jesus our Savior.

Divine Expectation

The life we hold to is sacred. It is a holiness of His expectation. That is what life is for us, Him.

Faith brings God. It is He that is that faith exists that we love God. By accepting ourselves as real persons, we know God by Him in love with us. He is the perfect compliment to the person we are, life. He brings us up to be, mature, and act, exercise what in Him we call faith.

When we know what is "being in God," we know life within that is "of us." Never is more less or otherwise. We are His creation. To know Him is in being so. We are indelibly mark His and likewise He is of us. It is that one is not apart but of each other. His creativeness is who He is and what we are.

Our very fabric that joins us is the creative faith we both are and yet because of differ.

Divine expectation is the predestined will of Him. We are that life, living and choosing to live. In such life, all is His expectation for us. It is a view of destiny—that we all share in Him. It is our blessed assurance we have of Him, trust and confirmation.

Joining Wills for Life

The truth of our living has groans and utterances that speak of life and the grave. We are vexed as human with the constant prospect of the turmoil in death.

Constantly, we reconcile it with faith, or lacking that, only in our own strength.

It is truth that speaks of our living out humanity.

God offers us hope in the faith of Jesus Christ.

The Spirit of God graces us daily with each new day of life. In this power, we are able to find hope in Christ. Nothing is possible in our own strength, only in His. Everything in humanity must be graced.

Tension Binds, the Spirit Frees

Some thoughts turn us tense. It is a shame to see discord. Peace is the rule. How else can we cope? To have serenity is to have found our real person.

We are meant to embrace not be in turmoil. Life is an easement for our dying. To be real is to accept a true notion for grounding so that we can step off in faith.

Thoughts like these validate our need for Christ. To step off our sorrows for Him is what dying is about. Death is every day we say we have had enough and reach to God.

Tension signals us a part of us is experiencing the rigors of death. Why not step off into Christ? There is life and a full restoration of us.

Thoughts need not find us times but in the freedom of His love.

Growing Old!

As times of old go, our life issues in new mannerisms—some fuller, some beginning in importance.

These gathering over time reflect our maturity. We are not alone, although time would indicate we are on a solitary faith.

Death is something for conviction, and our maturity says it will be a profoundly lonely experience. We die by ourselves as fate calls each forth to their terminal moment. Moment after moment passes, and lives pass from their solitary confinement in the earth.

The comfort of God is to know His host. We are not alone. The fates do not dictate death. God ushers us to the homeland of heaven.

Whatever view represents our level of faith or lack of it.

We have a choice. God is mine. Can you make a choice?

Coming to Him

Living is finding a cure for messes and an answer to death. Living presents us full of opinions and beliefs.

It is here faith enters. Here, God is a symbol of life's faith. He is its fruition.

The Lord places His trust in us so we can complete each day. His way is to bring forth truth in our life so that we can measure how He lies in us.

We want to be His, and this can only be if truly we lie within His interior.

When we think of the Lord, He amazes us with His sovereignty.

He brings us to a reality in Him that makes all His answer.

When He brings us within His fold, He cares so we are strong with anointing and grace. He wants us to extend His hand.

He hopes His mystery through us as mystic knowledge of life.

The times we enjoy with His Life are the transformation of our spirit.

Finding His Life in Spite of This One

How can we avoid God? Impossible? We are only mortal. He is almighty. When He calls, pride forms, not humility.

Our heart is biological and spiritual. Pride turns attention to us, not to the universe, Him. We think we are the universe and that He is distant.

Pride is the feeling that life is by our living.

Excluding His impact or the eternal by Him, we are doomed to this earth for we lack in faith.

God's task is to turn us into faith lovers. This is part of a mystery, predestination. It is not so important we walk with Him as admit His sovereignty over our souls.

Life is by His living through us. When we acknowledge Him, humility sets in and we are truly chosen.

He loves us, so we have life.

Our Choice

Life calls to us. Do we listen? It is the call of life's passing, saying all we know is fleeting. This is the nature of life. Jesus uses this work of His to bring us to Him.

Life speaks of death. We are faced with dimensions that are beyond us. We need God. We need God to reach beyond our limitedness. In God's creativeness of life, the impact of His sacred nature is more than we alone can handle.

Then we come to His promises. What is He saying? Are we unique in the fleeting of time or in the long view of eternity? What does new life mean, where eternal life follows this temporal one? All of this takes Jesus for an answer.

We are to have the aplomb accorded to godliness. We are lost to ourselves if not with true faith. We need to run to God. There is no other safe haven, only fear.

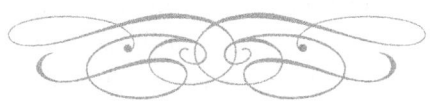

Being His Opportunity

To be in tune with God is to experience His opportunity. We all seem to be looking for it, and opportunity is His presence shining as life before us. Maybe we know Him as a neighbor, a friend, a loved one, etc. It matters not. Once we know Him, it is His knowing that transports us past a feeling to an experience.

His actualization deepens as ours.

The best we can purpose is to have His opportunity opportune us with each day. Then we shine transcendent within the life He knows us through.

This is what His presence will do—make us transcendent in the life we are but dust within.

The heart is moved so that we are an image to His goodness. Our soul reflects that glory is what life we live.

When we are His opportunity, we are real. So honest, pure in Him, we know the life—the life that is His making.

We are open as truth to Him. How can such not be opportune?

Feelings that Reveal God

Time crosses our path and we think. We are attune to the pulse of feelings—feelings that speak and challenge. They are our intuition of faith. The bringing of truth. Something about us and about life. Where we fit in and who we are.

Feelings so powerful they can change thoughts. Beliefs are just a deeper knowledge of us. God is knowledge that transcends and sets free.

Feelings are us interlaced with God.

Truth is accepting God as a word to feel and embrace so that thoughts believing in faith emerge. God lives as that word of life, for He speaks to our heart and soul. He is irrepressible to any thought or feeling we may have. He emerges faith in us.

His creativity is our excellent desire for the life in Him to be for us. To hold this life is to find our victory that we can feel love and know joy.

Love's Making

Love is tenacious. It pulls at our heart for us to do something so clearly defining in the public.

It talks of moments in time as if they will never be so keenly expressed and opportune.

We are those moments that God divinely brings into opportunity. He wants us to discover His eternity in us.

Love, between us, is the recognition of Him drawing us to act within His love for us.

He says life is a unity of who we are and Him, love. Love is so pure it makes us come to completion in Him. He wants us to realize what He has laid on the heart.

He calls life through us by opening Himself to us, revealing goodness that pulls virtue up within us. To be so poised with blessings is to be a garden which flowers His desire that we see ourselves as a beautiful creation set in the hope of His goodness.

Love is not what we make of it but what it makes of us. To see love is to be so much a blessing for our love.

Once and Passing

The taste of friendship is a conceit of pride. To be held in confines or reduced in ability is what makes the specialty of intimacy.

It is dictated through or abandoned.

In very clear hues, passions inflame to the purpose of self-oriented.

We cannot buy life on crumbs, or to be held in such a disposition.

Maybe we need a new honesty, not so power corrupt.

Weathering Storms

I am short of reason and emotional. My nature is toward deep and heavy. My inclination is to soften with fluff, but I cannot find steadiness.

The way I go, nothing will follow. I am uncertain and underutilized. Maybe I need an attitude readjustment, or maybe I am disappointed. Surely, a case of integrity is under weather. I need to focus on the life He has with me and carry it home.

It's really just me.

Finding God

What the Lord is for us is someone who consumes us. His love is what we call reality.

The love we bear is His life. We are to know life by how it changes us. We are void of reason here as faith divines us to Him. It is how love influences faith that all passes into Him.

In the passage of time, we exist for their eternity meshes with our soul.

The desire to be real places us in a view that brings about new change. It is a kind of change that respects us. It is a sign that the Holy Spirit has authority in our lives.

That authority says we are truly love. It is a love so deep it calls to the Master.

As we give life this part of us, God becomes for all of our life. We are driven to find God so we can find ourselves. He consumes us, so He is love.

Excellent Ways

In the corner of my mind comes the view of humanity. I see it in many ways expressing what is a lowering of excellent. We are too consumed with our ability and not with a vision of excelling which places us beyond our mind's eye.

God is the supreme good. All that is by way of virtue is in Him. Faith takes us to that place in us where He inspires.

That charge of faith takes us beyond mortality. The eternal road leads thorough countless blessing. We need not have reached our ultimate freedom to enjoy those blessings.

God brings us to heaven in faith by letting us know the inspirations of love. Love immortalizes us and makes us excellent in our ways.

Being Godly

On the forefront of making a good person is the ability of God to see goodness in us.

What we call a light is evidence of spiritual depth. Each of us carries a light. We need to let it shine for our life to come forth in our living.

We need to guide the inner life with godliness. Religion and science only establish our need. Walking in partner helps support the afflicted.

Each of us has a grace of life from which springs goodness. It is by having a focus on the present that grace opens the frontier of the future in our mind.

To fully live is to have an unconditional hope, one that means we have love in our heart that endures for hope.

Our Christian walk needs to be full, so we need basic faith.

Eternalizing Hope

The hope of life that Christ promises for us contains a fulfillment beyond eternity and salvation. It is the hope that beats in every man's heart.

There, the thread of eternal and temporal life pass through. Love that breeds up is there. It says who we are and that love is at essence within commingled with the essence of worldly life. Here is our option, to find faith or mediocrity.

We need to see love as our basis and its extension as being who we are. When we center our life as love, faith manifests by the hope of that love to see life as an adequate abundance of virtue to cast an expression of material wealth that is at peace with our heart. It takes faith to find virtue to hold peace for the heart, and we can find wealth to bring peace.

It is the nature of hope to be so blessing upon us. And it endures because we have found love.

Evangelizing

The mark of the Trinity is nature. It is upon our soul. God creates and so blesses us for good. The expression of that good is by the goodness we put into life.

What we want in life is the secure peace of ethical morality, something that necessitates the good result in life. That is God to the believer.

In the mind of the world, many means lead to that gate. Yet in God good in our lives is a blessing of virtues. We only begin to notice this with our life given to God. Every expression of our life reveals His goodness.

We are so blessed and yet acts of life and lives remain unredeemable. It is justice before our very eyes. Unsaved pagans and acts of the devil.

So blessed we are that our goodness touches and heals. The mark of the Trinity is shared by our life with others.

Cocreator

Mistakes proliferate. In someone's grace, we find our true intentions to rectify, repair, or replace.

In these intentions, life finds fulfillment in us. We answer questions of ability and aptness of focus and decisiveness.

How we deal with uncertainty in the face of habit. Change in habit shows our adaptability and level of maturity.

Where we are mentally when dealing in life is a statement of how our recovery is progressing.

We must be observant to reckon correctly with events.

We can't allow ambivalence. We need to be certain in the pursuit of goodness. Or our good fails to be certain.

Grace comes when we give it invitation.

His Love, Our Virtue

Love is pursuing the joy in God. We are that love. It is because God pursues us that we are. He pursues, so life is our existence. The more He follows us with life, the more we repent to discover Jesus. His life puts eternity in our heart and Him in our purpose.

We, His love, love to love. But as we notice, all people love. They may love to love, or love to hate, or love to be hurt. For whatever reason people love, they are His love. But He wishes for them simply to love, to extend to others what Jesus gives them.

Love is God's creativity for virtue. He gifts virtue as love and asks we give love as a virtue. Creativity is the handprint of God. Ours is to imitate in the nature we give pleasure. For His good is pleasurable, and that is what makes love a virtue.

An Empty Glass

There is a voice in us of this life that prompts us to the good and lofty in life. Some call it conscience. Some call it the Holy Spirit. Some see man's heroic nature through it.

Somehow, God leaves an imprint, an image of Himself upon man. Created from the earth. Given life by earthen vessels. Man is indeed. He shares a role with God.

God invites him into His perfection. Man chooses between the hills and the valleys, scarcely seeing the mountain and abyss coming into view.

Here, man stands on a precipice.
The voice speaks prophetically.
He hears, but does he understand?
Do any of us?

When the ethos of time passes, do we act in the truth of this moment or are we deceived? God listens for us. But is there anything?

Love Masters Despair

Events in this world are unexpected.

When we contemplate our blessings little, do we perceive they will be snatched up in a moment's notice?

Life and death are partners in our crime. We fail to see how sin follows us. Death is our fulfillment. It is the ecstasy of our despair.

God hears us in this. He calls to us with an answer of love.

To love as oneself the lives we pass in the desert of God's love. We are to be a love for Him and others. And letting this grace upon us from beyond us.

What gathers life is blessed so that love can be. And we love, so the quiet of despair can find the wholeness in us by the Christliness of our brokenness.

The Surrender of Grace

The joy of life is found in the excellence of Jesus's company. Here are find new life that is universal for peace and accord.

The dispensation of grace in our lives is the miracle works of God. The soul is given into glory to be given Christlike nature. It comes about when we empty our pride and accept new love, our rebirth. Pride is any glorifying of our humanity. We, in Christ, are led deeper and deeper into a selfless life of sacrifice. The more we do the, more life we enter in, and eternity becomes much more ours and Jesus's reality of life. We share in deeper fellowship.

As this life revolves in us, we are given to moments where our personal grace has a power to heal. And then we work with Christ. In His company, grace from us as a healing of this life into our new one.

Loving Him

We are destined to love. It brings us to perfection. It is God at peace. It is a melody of our desire to be. When we give love a moment, we are a universe of passion. What God does is bring us up to the divine cause for love.

The human cause for love is found in our suffering. Each of us desires a reconcilement of peace. So finally our will is dignified.

God does this mercy in each encounter.

Perfect reconcilement can only happen after God consumes us. That is the manifest desire we hold.

We are sensitive to our needs, and sometimes the boundaries of definitions seem blurred. But what the Lord wants for our life is ample cause to enter His life.

We need to see how perfectly He graces us.

It's called assurance. Isn't that what this life calls for? His life is assurance for eternity. We only have to let Him be Lord.

Justified to Love

We need to justify our faith occasionally, and there's Jesus.

Then we have hearts of unconditional faith for Him. And when we extend this gift to these in the shadows, light comes.

We all come to a purifying test of faith. To see if we are entirely in surrender to Jesus. The shock will have us either cling to Jesus or to the world.

We come to moments our heart needs to eclipse in faith. We need to build our heart in Christ, and all that brings us to Him. All, just to come into empathy for those suffering in the shadows.

They need a healing beyond our knowledge, perhaps even beyond this life. But not our prayers.

We need to be a rock of piety for Jesus. There, He can bring a godly response out of us.

We need no anxiety. Just the Spirit of love.

Our Woundedness Defines Us

We come to nexuses in the road of life that brings us to great union with others. What the Lord has done to bring such interchange in His body is the miracle of His writing. We can see, with them, the simple truths we are bound by.

Woundedness only allows us entry into each other's heart. There is a pasture green with life. That is the difference. For some, their heart is barren. For others, it is lush with life. There, He is planted.

Woundedness appears when we allow the heart to suffer in spite of what may heal it. We suffer for some apparently good emotional reason. There never is any.

Emotions are a safety value for the peace of the heart. Misused, they shield the heart and prevent growing and maturing. They then stagnate it.

The heart is always poised to God, ready for healing.

Only we may not be.

What comes to terms with God suffers too, our soul. It fails to know God for the light He is to us.

Finding Oneself

What happens so surely is our coming of age.

We wander in our spirit to our own consternation.

Finally comes the time when everything gels.

God wants us to be real, true to who we are. Until we find who we are this can never take place.

Love is the perfect intercept between Him and us. When this is the case, we can find ourselves.

Being charismatic is just that case.

Otherwise, finding ourselves means finding ourselves clutching problems and not blessings. Our sense of esteem for this life is reduced, and we do not get the approval we so desperately seek.

Only God can give this to us.

When we do find Him and us in love, we see as He does and we know the Holy Spirit.

What Love Calls Us To

God calls; we are made into Him. Glory is that life He has us enter in. It is the pressing of the divine and human into the oneness of His Spirit.

How much we have asked to be a part in destiny, our destiny. Love is what forms it, so we are perfect in Him and not in the nature of earthly limitedness. We go beyond the infinite to find the eternalizing of life, Christ's very own nature.

The determination of God is in every act of love we possess. In that determination, we come into Christ emblazoned with loving so He is alive and we are.

We are blessed to Him. He calls so the soul is reborn of the heart. In Christ, life is the emblazoned love we are to carry as mission. Life means Jesus is alive, and so we are blessed. Life is the love that convicts us.

So eternal we are as convicted love. That is destiny—to be open so His love is us being convicted of God.

In Our Heart

In the peace of the moment is the heart of His people. The way of truth bears upon all. He is in all and so we are in Him.

The sensitive nature of the heart exceeds any direction we may enter. It is the nature of divine life bringing redemption. The heart can only be changed as humility brings cause to God for grace upon us. It is spirit having cause upon us as a vitality of life.

The life engendered is what Christ is for each.

Christ lets the heart open to revelation and in so, our imperfections of heart get to be made whole within as.

To be so perfected is to know what many call as being imperfect of the heart.

God never makes without purpose to bring us to call within Him.

Whatever our disability, He calls us to life to bring dignity and virtue to it to place this love we call like into His glory.

First, we must find it, so He can glorify the cross with it.

The Cross We Bear

Each day we walk, our cross develops. It is loving, not shaming. It stands as a banner of love between us and our God.

In it is our heart and soul of incarnate love. He shows us how it brings us closer to Him.

Examining our conscience lets the Holy Spirit bring greater definition to it. It never leaves us but embraces life. And with that, we share in His victory.

How we get into this life is immaterial to what we allow God to be for us. Our cross lovingly reminds us each day is His way, and we are in it by the faith of His seed.

People with a burden find it mesmerizing so that they only can see life by it. We need to see the naked truth before us, not colored by another or its influence. It has a way of growing in their eyes before them when they should see the Christlike nature of life developing before them.

Our cross leads to victory if we give Him our burdens.

Recovery Is a Manner of Life

There is an abode. It calls to the weary. It makes us free of burden. It is where we find the solace of the heart. Here we are. Here we be. It is easy to beat peace.

It reflects a healthy view of one's recovery. In this manner, the ends of relationships are neatly tied. Nothing is obscure.

The language is crisp and alive. Functionalism is over.

Now the maker of one's history stands poised, to engage, be of merit, and be lost in living. Life is a proud moment we wish always to be the maker of.

The deciding factor is, is your will in agreement with what you decide? Without it, growth is impossible. You then tend to flower with no reward.

In my eyes, I see how the clock of time can slowly, but inextricably advance one, if they are in agreement with true earnest nature of hope before one's eyes.

Salvation

Love comes for each of us in the nature of our life.

What takes place restores miracles. It is a growing. A showing of power. That life be set free to Christ. Aging.

Here, life gathers and extends. A step. A stage of faith.

It is what takes us beyond.

We no longer suffer but live. In equivocal balance. Love tempers the spirit and brings the soul to a healthy release.

Love brings us to ourselves. Reality.

It is how simple feelings propel thoughts. To be so blessed is covenant. Godly. An icon from God.

Something innate and sacramental. It is His mystery. We live it. Yet so feebly do we see it.

The Ground We Find Recovery

The revealed life is a thought that comes as the nature of all life. Here is the creative source, the living that is a paradigm of us.

It shows how recovery works for us.

When it comes, the ground of intent must be firm. Then vision is that transcends time, which emanates from the soul.

If we look on how recovery is, it makes us know our maturity toward any completion. To examine us so is to equate what life becomes by our entry and how fulfillments line up for us. It is in researching life's making that we discover how far fulfillment proceeds in any direction with us.

It begins by simply viewing the creative genius in any event and how we are drawn. Then using that genius to fulfill. There is no end point, only where we wish to end it. Construction like this is a matrix of recovery.

Authority Comes from Being That Is Real to Each

Recovery means we explore the ways given to us to assess issues and deal with events. An issue is something that we find our answer through relationships of life. Events are the kinds of circumstance of our living. Both show recovery. For it is where our life and its living show us areas of betterment we have authority over.

Salvation shows where God's faith of us allows Him to bring our heart and soul into greater sanctity with Him. We are improving in ways we have no authority over. The covenant in God keeps us in a sacrificial relationship that is based on His authority over our lives. What He leads us into, as long as we do what He asks, we are to follow. It means faith is the means and not our strength.

The abundant life is not just the manifestation of His salvation for us, but also the acting in concert we make as recovery. It is the well-being of a relationship that makes for authority.

His Virtue

In the interim between us and His consumption of us lies the experience of tried out virtue.

Where we hold firm to Him, we are in virtue with Him. We have the connection but not a nexus with Him when that isn't the case. It's all up to grace. Yet He wants us completely as His and not in spirituality alone.

This can only happen as this life gives way to His.

Within virtue of Him, we literally employ His image to overcome the law. It is in this process we grow in image as the perfection of our love approaches unconditional focus.

As virtue is tried, we fail and sin. Only through the process of reconciliation are we healed and cleansed. Then the process begins in new virtue of Him, until finally we are consumed into love as materially we surrender, not just spiritually.

Faith that Burns of Love

The passion of His faith squarely places our heart ablaze of the truth of Him, commitment.

The fire of our faith determines how well we give Him access to our life. His desire is for us to love Him as He loves us unconditionally.

We place into faith what calls for His attention. What is left is ours. Why do we want this ownership? Surely, we would prefer to handle what He sees fit for us and not to hold onto what should be in His hands. Faith calls for a complete surrender of our life to Him, so He can bless us in the knowledge of what forms our life and not to the contrary.

Our faith walk is the extent we have knowledge of Him in our lives. To grow in faith is to grow in the knowledge of God for your life. For where you know of God in your life, there is where you have allowed Him passion in your, faith.

He calls us to faith. He causes our heart to burn so purely it brings love. It is faith that calls us to Him when love is in the heart.

My Faith

My desire is to be filled with life to pursue His quest for my heart. He wants me to be in His faith with all of my soul. The value of my life is incumbent on how clearly faith brings me to Him.

To be so focused each day is giving Him what is in knowledge of faith in Him. Trying to be open to His desires for me.

In focusing on Him, I have a chance to be more by Him. The knowledge of Him is the awareness of life each day brings. It is an experiential activity. Something only one in process is truly open to.

We wish to be gifted, fruitious, and blessed. But all I want is completion in Him.

My quest is His design. Salvation purses a road only He knows.

It is a road to test faith, challenge the heart, and let the soul soar. One can only be assured of the limits of possibilities in the Lord, no limit at all.

Being One

When we discern what life is, it all comes from His essence. It is love. Any discernment that shows the believer's heart and not God's is false.

Judgment is not to shelter bias but to bring people into a real love. It is not to kill them with attachments but rather to free them of them.

There was a time before the Holy Spirit made God indwelling. Then justice was based on a legal covenant and not an indwelling one.

Thus, this age of grace requires us to apply a grace with love when we act through our convictions.

This is the deepening of the process of His life, to draw us closer so we can together be His Church and not scattered.

The devil will have no part in us finding His love. All of us are His love. Separate, we will not grace glory.

Touching So Life Forms

Once time and space are no more, we are in the eternal hands of God. We are blessed to know life in Him. We are no longer given to attachments of the flesh. We have a place in God; He calls to us with it. He never lets us be condemned. Our restoration is complete.

Where duty and honor fall short, grace provides.

Our purpose is to discover our heart. To let Christ feel us within our very being. To be so led our very feelings and impulses move to His touch.

To be a church in God is to have vision. He brings for us to see. To see the revealed life of God in us and in all being we are. It means taking vision for life, so we can accept Him as an entirety of all of us. That is church.

We walk so in His touch.

To have such glory shine as us is to hold our heart for His blessing, a hiss of life.

Salvation Has Grace toward Recovery

Recovery is us in the notice of God. It happens every day. He sees us stumble, and He turns it into a good we will never know until we reach glory. All human activity is stumbling. On our own power, we are insufficient. Grace keeps us to God. It makes all possible through God by being in grace.

He turns stumbling into virtue by His grace to have all life in Him. When we hold Him in faith, He makes grace give way to covenants.

But before we are examined in faith, we exist in Him for to live it to be in grace of His life.

In recovery, there is linkage to salvation. In bettering one's life, one becomes better to God, salvation.

The Promise of Love

God, the servile nature of obedience comes to us.

All of life begs to be loved. A promise. A promise is what love is. To be and act differently, that is our promise if loved. Love will change the heart.

God wants to love us if we will let Him in. He wants us to love so we will know He doesn't change as He changes us with His love.

It is classic in showing who is that love becomes him, God, and how we change to come as Him, into the promise of love. It is someone we know as our nature—to be like Him.

When love enters, there is life. God is present. We can only be men of His integrity. The promise of love speaks. We are transcendent and alive. God shows Himself. We are real. The power of God is a message of His promise.

We keep His promise.
The love given is the knowledge of God.

A Fall from Grace

When we go from faith to reason or feelings for or way to truth, truth no longer has a life by revelation but by legalisms.

We destroy the fullness of hope. Grace is not a human condition; it is a supernatural life. God is then depicted by our imagination.

When faith is not the issue, then we lack dignity to live; the righteousness of Jesus Christ will not reach us; we are too blind by our own pride.

The person balanced by reason or emotions will lack the uplift of faith to take them to lofty ground beyond the human pathos and base value.

In reason, one will construct arguments of logic highly critical of the heart.

In feelings, one will make flighty pursuits of emotion our validation of truth.

In both, it is the strain developed by a kind of work that distinguishes a truth, not unconditional love, all truth.

He Is Alive and We Are Well

What we need is knowing that is the fervor of Jesus Christ's heart. We need to know life, His life and how it passes in us.

To know the merit of living, life is to be an eternal moment, something Jesus wants of us.

To be an eternal moment means letting God have our surrender. It means standing in one eternal moment for Him. To let open a door for the eternalizing of us. Just one moment. That's all it takes. To give freely with no reservation to the eternal, the river of living water, the Holy Spirit.

Jesus perpetuates the Holy Spirit in our completing surrender. It is in His love the Spirit finds us open and unashamed.

Finding Jesus is a perennial mystery. That is the eternal, a quest that renews and never quits renewing.

In that renewal, we are opened to His life, so He is alive, and we are at peace.

Shaking Despair Free

For God to take despair from us, we must learn to love God, so our relationship pales anything else. We cannot entertain a relationship with more grace than we have with God. Then when we grace Him more, He can take despair from us because we do not value it more than all, God.

God is not despair but love. When we love Him more, we love despair less, and He can move it from us.

First is to know if we do want to get free of our despair. Or if we have some hidden agenda concerning it.

For each of us, there is the cross for us to let go of things.

Despair pits us against our graced lives. God frees us when we love Him.

Longer than Life

The mountain is deep and the sea wide that the Lord covers. We are on that hill and on that pond. All that the Lord holds looks larger than life. It is the revelation of His life existing therein.

We are larger than life for to the Lord we exist in faith. And His faith sees the righteousness of Jesus. Larger than life.

That is Christ. Larger than our life. And when we forget or deem our life by comparison, we are lost. We need that blessed humility; the faith He bestows upon us is a composite gift of grace for our free will to find how to submit to God.

Faith in God is bigger than any eternity. He is the sum of all eternities. He is larger than life when we admit Him into ours.

When we give our life to faith, all is larger than life, for all becomes a manifestation of Jesus Christ. Our life holds s, but only Jesus is the sum total.

Recovery 3

The way we reconcile is a lot of how we pray. It is in the resolve to find peace that this is carried out.

I'd prefer a way to bring me to be perfected in Him, but I'll just settle with a common ground in Him.

I don't want to be a victim.

I've got to rediscover my impatience. It got to be graced with indecision.

It means being poised to surrender and know life lasts as long as it is not my expectation. When I give in to that expectation, everything is all right.

The gift of recovery is that we lack perfect control, but that faith perfects what has no good control.

I want personal success.

The Rising of the Lord

The risen Lord is upon us each time believers gather in faith. For He exists as there is faith to believe. We believe in faith for things from Him. Why not for Christ Himself before us. And as faith brings the grace of God to bear on the physical, why not Him?

He is a confirmation of belief. His body is faith—the faith of His body. We do not test with the mind but the heart. The spirit is guided by the Holy Spirit, whose presence stands as a witness of the risen God.

We do not put on blinders to life but see His giftedness within it. This comes with great discernment. Discernment which makes us open to His revelation.

So if you pray, He truly is so intimate and real as we say we have faith.

Love is the essence of faith, and He is the essence of love. Find Him. Don't be blind.

Truth, Real…So Real It's Elusive

There is a truth living in us that allows us to express this life in undeniable ways. Regardless of circumstance or relationship it exists. It is the knowledge based on our human qualities. It allows us to share within empathy.

With this expression of our human living come consequences we find ourselves affected by emotions and our thoughts. It is never a clear thing this living truth we wish to express.

Out of our deepest sincerity, our wounded brokenness wishes to speak this truth. The message may be strong. But it takes even greater strength to present balance.

Patience to rest upon the Lord for balance is our greatest strength. Then light shines in our heart upon the truth.

Being with Is His Stillness

In between our moments, God causes our life to be with Him. He separates our nature in those moments as godly or ungodly. It is a sign of our surrender to Him.

In our walk come moments of quiet despair when we find ourselves in a process of relinquishing to His surrender something that peaks as a loss or emptying of what we would call reality for His reality.

At the times the life we give over to Him seems a match for the life we gain in His reality.

Ultimately, we may be a part of His great stillness, where pervading holiness holds our wills together. Such a oneness frees us to act in His conscience. We are set free to Him in all manner of circumstance, in actuality and faith. Now reason discerns the logic of faith.

It means our prayers walk in the very life we are in His Life, and that they come true by how we set Him free into reality.

By how we submit. He finds honor in us.

Imaging Truth

The answer to life is in how we address and carry through it. It is a view that never alters, although our perspective to it may vary. Life is a constant flow of energy between us and God. A flow that may be in various forms, all pointing to the source which we may find ourselves through.

It is in this relation of life giving and life-bearing that we see the wonder of it all. Us, in cosmic grace uplifted to God of the universe. Such a scene impoverishes us within His majesty. But He calls to us by name, so that logo is an appellation we live with likeness.

Our limitations are only wellsprings for His grace to magnify into glory. We are such endeavors that light is pale through us unless so magnified. Then we emulate the divine in the pure truth we shine. It happens every time we let Him give our time a pull to eternity.

Such devotion is the living of life by detachment of personal glories and the definition of unconditional purpose, the love of all our ages, God's divine nature. Being a lamp for all.

Being Free Legally

When we grow in a family, tradition is cast through generations to us. We accept a role conceived in personality as the package of meres accepted in our families.

We become mature and legalistic all in the same motion. The only way we can affect this legalism is to pursue His Spirit, not who we are a mind, will, and emotion. They only add to the legal battle. We need something beyond ourselves, an infusion of the supernatural.

Being an image in life is limiting if we do not have life in us that overcomes that image. Making Him real by our personality is the way to go.

Our role shapes freedom and value.

Only God can make it work in us.

Being Graced

My heart is to know how to love with fullness of life.

It is in my intent to be a revelation. In doing this, God becomes immanent; I become one.

The journey I make is knowing God, so life in through one. My life is in glory. There I know God. To be so transcendent is to act with grace.

To know life effuses from our desire to have the good prosper is grace.

To extend this faith is to act with grace.

Loving with the fullness of life is the gifting of His grace.

Love works so we can live. Life is the total of our living.

Grace is the sum of all life.

The Well-Handled Vessels

When we give of our fullness, nothing but the charismatic happens.

What is mystical is subdued. What is material is spiritual. He loves us in our relationship. We are His art, simply for His pleasure.

In the way He receives us so we are empowered in our dedication's surrender. If we desire more, we must heed His preparation, testing, of us. For He is so pure, only if not aware of Him we cannot detect how immediate He is.

In our life, we never make a move to Him; He makes all motion in the spiritual except for our complete surrender before Him. Sometimes, surrender is a lifetime or a death or what may be more. It means our soul has His image. For those whom surrender comes within life, theirs is the completion of reason to discernment.

Everything is a transformation or healing.

It is the awareness and its openness to it. He is our openness that brings awareness.

We are made by His touch. We need to have Him complete us with His touch.

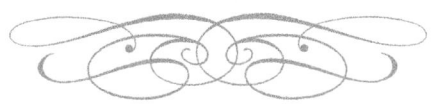

His Cross's Consuming

If we are not put to the cross, then is it just a relic we drag around. If it does not mean a deepening of our Christlike nature, then what do we share with Jesus? An exercise of faith.

Certainly, our faith is not an empty ritual but alive in Christ.

The meaning of the cross is to bring closer insight of our death and where it will take us. We can never realize the price we will pay for our faith, but in faith, we can surrender it to Christ who will lead us through. His mystery that will culminate in our ascension.

To think our life is the price and the reward is incalculable, and yet Christ makes all things possible.

The Holy Spirit reveals all this to us if we just unstop our ears and listen. We need to cure ourselves by giving pride over to humility.

His Love

In the course of things, we come to a conclusion of meaning for us.

We are destined to romance His life into eternity. There will be our true form, something only Christ could love. So refined we become, only His love brings the betterment of goodness by us. We are His to move and cause to being. He loves us, so we accept what will He may have for us.

What we may know by timeless romance is what a splendor life is. We cannot hold forms to their shapes. We cannot expect Christ to us always. But we can know He will never give up giving us love.

We can only humor ourselves with great principles. But it only comes down to love. Who do we love? Christ? When we give up on love, we give nothing good. Love is the exchange we find in having being.

Where there is being, Christ brings us to love. Love so dear it reveals the Father.

Love and death are the legacies of life. God lets us choose one.

Pastoral and Alive

Once we walk with Christ, life opens up to us. We can see how He is the daylight to our darkness. In this lush field of devotion and service, we come into our own Christly nature. Here we find God so supremely good and true. Where argument enters so dovetails faith. We are not alone.

In this verdant pasture, He leads us to peace so we can have that blessed assurance. We are overcome with this ecstasy. With trembling, we offer Him surrender daily, to fill us for what He removes.

When we can pray for the salvation of all, then we truly have holiness and not worldliness. When we walk with someone, there is empathy. If we say we need Him, then how much more transparent we are of Him.

The pastures of faith are where we eat His flesh and blood. Here we are real to Him. Each day we surrender is such a pasture. Each time we surrender, He feeds our soul His revelation, until we are not lacking in grace.

And so do we become the fruit of Him.

Gospel

Sometimes, there's an overwhelming tide. Then there comes the time to regroup to force time's next tidal force.

We cannot be certain until the wind no longer rages against the earth. We cannot hear the truth with the winds of gossip against our ears.

The key to the door with truth lies in the ring of keys that has no shame. It is the self-righteous that comes forward. The key to truth is humility.

It takes the eyes of the spirit to see the unseen. Our heart remains locked. Only the key of truth will give us audience to what we desire.

Truth discloses not by reason but by love. The better the love, the more truth. Being real is that truth. Being real is honesty and courage.

And that is our choice.

The Garden of His Love

My heart beats for the truth of God. His love. His hope. His joy. That is truth. Truth that lives. It lives to give me life.

This is the love of God, His truth.

We cannot, who are in love, do anything in passion but in the Spirit of Jesus Christ.

We look to life to nourish, guide, and fit us to live. Only God's love can.

The Maker has only good things for us. Love in His desire. We are that love is, so we can have life.

Life is the meaning of love—from God to our despair, lonesomeness, hurt, and emptiness. It returns us to a garden with God. Sin tries to put an end to that vision, so we are truly lifeless.

Revealing His Incarnation with Us

Life is the fulfillment of being. It takes one to where inclination becomes activity. It is where faith emerges from the quiet. It is the nature of quiet. Why so much in darkness comes into the light is because it is in quiet, not turmoil.

In the stillness, God exists alive for Him to emerge in our faith through the test of circumstance. He waits to help the unsuspecting soul. If we were to anticipate Him, we would no longer admit ourselves to His faith but our sight.

It is the nature of mystery to cloak us.

It is a gradual and steady revealing of truth.

It is the perfect teacher.

In seeing Christ or the incarnation that transfigures us into God, Jesus is more by our human nature. This kind revelation assures us of God and His design.

His Will

What happens to us is fated of God if we are truly in Him. When we become co-redemptors, then our will lies with the importance in His will in determining our fate.

For us not to partner with God seems strange to some. Yet if we feel there is oneness in our will, then God surely determines our fate. For how can we change God's perfect will? And would we ever want to?

What happens to us then is a mystery, something tied up in revelation we can never fully know, even after it has past. That is God's will, higher.

We can ask if truly God is in command with all that takes place. Yet if we love God, then we will know by faith all is in His will, and it is perfect sovereignty.

Faith Is God's Liberty for the Living

For all we can do, nothing matches living in faith. So much joy and hope transpire. It means freedom for those captive in the bondage of the world and its ways. Enter God and our godliness to Him.

It means being changed up to give. We are not indulgently prone on what we can receive or have in ownership. For the world possesses us by our ownership. It is a very different thing than being in the care of or acting as stewards.

To know we are in the heart is to know the way the heart beats with His love. To know this is to understand faith and its operation of us. When we are gifted by God, the gift is what makes who we are. We do not possess faith. Rather, God submits us to Him through it. He gives it to us to use to know Him, but it is God who knows us so that faith can be our liberty of the possession we are, even without it.

The Mystic

Jesus comes as the incarnation of our hopes, all our hopes.

Every day, He is there pointing grace upon the inequity of our hopes. It is a pouring of salvation. We are in the limits of recovery. He is in the infinite freedom of our life. Somehow, the two are one.

This is Jesus in me. The infinite lies hidden in me, and the limited nature of me remains clear in the open. Somehow, the hidden joins with that in the open, us. It is us in the image of Jesus. He is the incarnation, Jesus Christ.

That is what recovery is, bringing incarnation to our lives as faith brings us to virtue in our having clay natures.

Jesus is that in us that sees both the recovery human and the salvation divine. It is a calling, not problem solving.

Meditations

There is something to the gradual merging of His life with ours that shows in the rare nature of the friends He brings us into.

It's here He does the most of our healing for character and heart wholeness.

The Holy Spirit is our love, and relationship shows this as true.

The love in friends is a desire for the bride-groom, Jesus.

Here we find His simplicity for us. Whether it be in the sublime or subtle, He is there. All of life becomes our experience of His life upon us.

All of life becomes a ritual of our primary relationship, alive as the love of the heart. The ecstatic love is ours to contemplate life if we just allow Him, give Jesus a sovereign life upon us.

We are all part of His creative arm, bringing it to life.

Relics Original to Christ

We are all carrying relics that join us to Christ. Our cross is a relic of Jesus. It symbolically stands for how each of us has a gospel walk that joins us into the holy cross of Jesus. Yes, it is a relic we carry of the mystery of Jesus's crucifixion symbolically presented to us in faith. It helps us see the life of Christ in others. For from this symbol come our convictions of faith that the Holy Spirit has laid within each of our hearts.

It is as if we were in communion with the Lord Jesus. If we moved or went somewhere else, wouldn't we still be in communion? And so it is with the cross. We are compelled to hail Him wherever the cross is raised over us. And thus, we discover the unity of the Spirit, in the mystery of His faith. And here, our faith joins into His to make the greater mystery of the incarnation.

Here we are with a truth of His mystery in our lives when together we form a greater truth by the joining of mystery. Jesus is alive for us if only we are real to Him.

Being So Human

When we face each issue of concern, we see it fades into a series of expectations, an agenda if you will.

Then we see how priceless some negative feedback really is and how limited it is to derailing what mere actions can't account for, our self-esteem.

Self-esteem is based on one idea, you were born human and so is intrinsically unique. Now we try to say we can gauge that uniqueness based on your ability to work. The fact of the matter is that work is just one aspect of that uniqueness, which is comprised of indelible evidences within us.

The way one thinks or emotes. The evidence of faith. The gauging of the ability of one to work totally negates what one is doing besides work when one works. A human being is a complex of self-esteem; undermining it simply lowers the worth of all human.

When we want to humble someone, we must remember it's a gift of coming real before others. A gift only God can bestow.

Goodness that Flows of the Spirit

What we need to see is action transformed by the Spirit. Where there is faith centered on God action takes place to grace our life. It is no longer a concept of doing good but being transformed by the goodness to hold new faith in the assurance of God in all our life. To be so poised in life or to accept faith in God for all we call into our living.

It is when our willingness is a surrender to all His goodness.

This means there is an abundance from which we partake that will always be His goodness. Service that holds to His universality is goodness that can never fall outside of His will. Who are chosen to a life within Him. And all is concurrently good as a result.

Goodness is the measure of God. And that is where we are. In His goodness.

Goodness is service that holds to His desire for life. To be so as one, in union with God, that is His desire.

The love of the Lord will direct the Spirit upon us.

Our Life

The desire of the Lord is the unity of His Spirit. He says life is not ours to find but to be. To be so created that we are real. Reality is not our guide but unconditional love.

In time, faith is a concept. In eternity, it is the perfection of love. To be blessed so is to have eternity perfected.

As we are, life enters and carries Him to us.

To exist means we love Him for that is who we are to Him. In Him, we fly. Eternity is the blessing of Him every day. The gift we are is a measure of how God makes us love Him in the relations we have.

That life can only be a passing of time is how His life is choice of us by Him forever. As I am in Him, the world resonates a music sweet that brings recollection of Him. When we have a day in Him, mercy is more the rule, and our patterned behavior is less.

The baptism of this life we accept is our sign of faith.

Made with His Creativeness

One day, we shall see things all in a right fashion.

For now, we have to deal with bits and pieces of images.

My expectations have me led to the belief that better is conceivable. Only for me, an issue of time is necessary to bring all to a focus.

I am sure the essence of human greatness will descend upon me and heal me.

I am looking for a star without a constellation, then I will have found my light.

Likely, I will fall and lose my way. Where the light shines, there is my heart.

The arch to human success starts the tunnel of personal change. Only by reaching into the depths of our being is this possible. And when it is made, you cannot be undone.

The trick is to die for living.

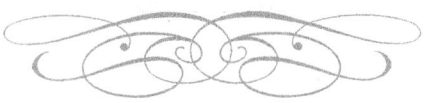

His Life in View

When we are lofted high, we see how beautifully He causes us to His life.

Such is how salvation stretches us to be a part of a causeway to the eternal and bridge our soul past death into His life.

To have such vision is to see in the Spirit of God.

We are merged into Him by the purity of faith we have of Him. It is how perfectly we take His faith in us and let shine love for Him in faith. The more is a gaining of our perfection.

As we go deeper *in* Christ, He opens us like a gift for Jesus. Something so pure and handsome to His touch.

We are shaped to be unconditional as love in Him.

Inspiration is Him letting us find Him in the eternal.

What God Says?

The turning of events in life makes God speak to us. It is the meaning of our walk to be the message of incarnate love. To be partner with God in His revelation.

Where life leads to is a deepening or saturation of our spirit. It is grace abounding in us. We extend it within blessing or covet it as curse. That is the nature of spiritual health.

The idea of becoming embraces what view God has with us. Our openness to His mind is desired if we are to have Him grow in revelation.

To hear God is to let our becoming heart be in faith so that life is expressed as eternity.

God never means to withhold life at death but use it to serve as a moment He is in ascension that we can be lifted into triune bliss.

Finding God

When we give freely, He says blessed be the persecuted for heaven shall bring them to Me.

As we walk alone with God, He shows life to be holy and just. And that we are people of life. His love sends us into further pursuit, that ecstasy He hides in.

I am in the nature of God, love, and being so finding at essence God alive in me.

He calls so purely that more is the simplicity of heart and less is who we are.

We need strength and courage of conviction to see faith in Him through all.

My view of Christ is to let be what holds life and embrace the heart of Him who lets this life be this image of His greatness. What I hope for is for man to unshackle his fear and be the prayer of God's hope for humanity. We can see that in Christ. But do not all of us issue forth in salvation seeking Him in all life.

We need so God can be. We want so we are also.

Love Transcends Us

The love we are is the love we have. When we receive, it is in giving that the honor to us of that love comes through.

In giving love, one reveals how they know God. Giving and receiving love shows how God knows us.

Revealing the facets of our relationship to God and to others is an epiphany of our laudable humanity, godliness. Our relationship to God and to others is one. We see God in them and them in God when we are in relationship. It is a means for a covenant.

Covenant in relationship means love exists in an honor to each that is a determination in their part to promote the lasting of their good over any evil. To do so this good, they promote first as an extension of the very good that God is.

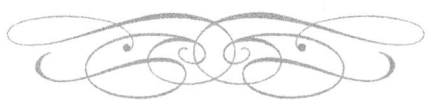

His Love

When in the din of activity, we find ourselves it will be a view of God. The nature of love is for it to wait upon us. It waits until we are ready. It is when our heart has a softening, a place for God to emerge into our life.

He waits with love for us. It is for us to explore His majesty, creation, our heart, and God. Here, we are released into the freedom of His Spirit.

The Lord has us in mind. His love is. His essence upon the dying heart. We are catapulted. Eternity becomes our heart the more He touches. It is the immortality of His divinity upon us, incarnation.

Each time, it leaves us with a choice of His will. To agree is His life by the sacrifice of ours.

Knowing Jesus

When we give full view to what God has done in our lives, then we begin to know Him.

Our contact with Him is the prayer of our life. By it, He knows our condition. In our daily effort and thoughts, this prayer is formed each day so that our life may come close to His. It is faith imaging us into Him.

For whatever reason, we fail ourselves. It is not because of insufficient grace in God. Instead, God gives us sufficient grace to succeed. For even when we fail ourselves, we succeed in God. We never fail with Him. He is the bright sun in our heart each day. Faith turns Him into the Son of God, Jesus. But that is only us clearly seeing His revelation. He is always with us.

But only if we have faith in Him do we know.

It means accepting life, all that He is to us.

Grace that Brings Life

To know life goes on is the epithet at a dirge.

We pick where we will call life or death. It is in the grace of our life these are made.

Grace is the collected thoughts, feelings, emotions, and sensations that are a part of anything we experience. God can make something good of our grace or we can command control over our cross and decide something humanly to do with this interior of us.

So for each of us is the experience of a dirge and the accompanying grace in all of us.

In the ensuing days, grace forms the shapes of beauty, ugliness, and myriad of countenances. It is when this countenance is of God we have touched upon our dignity of life, reality. All else is a reflected fantasy of grace, until faith is the revealing of life, not the human nature of grace but somehow divine.

She Line

The line that life inscribes with us is neither a reference for negative or positive, but a balance we live in as it sways the focus of life more upon and less upon.

It's a measure of the give and take of relations in respect to the relation we live in with ourselves.

Here, the soul and heart manage. They lead me to a greater affinity of God. Both make Him more so as our focal point of balance draws our life to greater relation. By having more connectiveness, we come into greater completion of conversion.

The line of balance shows the nature of our conversion. Either it is vital or lacking. Each condition states whether we have found God or are still seeking Him.

When our line measures conversion, it changes to show how golden we are. It is a transforming rule. We form a golden rule for others to see.

We show what we hold as faith for God to hold us.

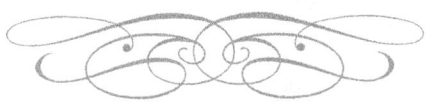

Who We Are

With dialogue comes the power of words. It is not argument but enrichment.

It takes us from our view to a new place—a place of trust and love. Here, our nature shines a reality of new creativity and liberation. We are in the grace of God. We grow to splendor as truth is clothed in beauty.

Memories are experiences that process this truth.

Our path is to take in the present and bring with it the past to a vision of the future. We find what involves us to bring hope to our life. Christ is at the focus of our vision. To see how the divine takes our love beyond ourselves and returns it with meaning.

We need to be real, true to ourselves. This is the basis to being Christly. God wants us to discover His creativity upon us, the man of faith we are.

Progressing as Life

The passage of time is an ugly event upon a person. It means there is a loss and debilitation of life. Maturing means are overcome by the ravages of age. What once was in grasp has been lost. The change we undergo means a further stepping of moral integrity for moral rigidity. We will always be, never as flexible as before. The plus side is, we can now stand up on our moral conscience.

We are now a person in responsibility and motive.

What we must do is go beyond our emotions to a baseline thought, comprehend what we lay upon our heart. In so doing, we can prevent distortion within us that works out through us.

In this way of addressing life, we come to know what is virile and constant within us. Something unspoiled by evil.

It is the divine presence of life.

We only can give life dignity and thereby find our beauty, His image of us.

Destined

What we are are creatures living a mortal issue that asks if there is more to what we call life than we know. We can only ascertain if the day is good or not. Beyond that, and maybe even in that, cultural anecdotes are with us.

It is a mystery by which we keep ourselves. To be human is to be caught as earthly yet manifesting into the eternal. In this connection to the eternal comes the legacy of our life. This is forged in a process we know through faith. Here, we show the heart that ultimately sends our soul to a way beyond time. There becomes our legacy.

It is an example of what shows, that living all comes into a greater measure of life. This fullness of life transports us past mortality to our immortal destiny. It is not merely being remembered as a lasting memory that is immortal by us.

We send our essence on a cosmic ride that irrigates and nurtures life throughout the universe. I call it being eternalized in Christ. He is our vehicle to surpass mortality.

The healing of eternity is the reward of unconditional love.

A Vision for Life

When time travels, we are beckoned to follow. Eternity calls to us but is not so readily seen.

When time enters our life, we give special notice of what is at stake. In eternity, our focus is on the Lord. We drift between both visions.

As we walk into His life, a convergence takes place. We see God in all circumstance as we continue to trust in Him.

The value of our vision is in what we give an indication of life's reality. Whether we see one perspective or another is not so vital as to how fully we engage in that life. God views us through the fullness of His life. How the two meld is His mystery for us. That is our walk of faith.

The fullness of our life is a result of which spiritual virtue comes into play for most of our life. That is the fullness God looks upon us through. When we look in this life, we know God.

The Community of Christ

We see in every heart of the godly a unity of spirit. Here, Christ dwells to secure assurance in each of their lives.

When Christ brings us to community in Him, the bandings of division and individuality must recede and exit from the heart. For Christ asks us to be brothers and sisters to each other, all part of His divinity by being a part of His family.

That is the operative word, family. To be blessed means to share blessings. To be cursed is to curse the covenant bond we share. When one prays, he is praying for all. Individuality is a secular notion, and division is from the devil. When one becomes more Christlike, all join Christ in a fresh glory.

The lowest servant of God raises the standard of Christ. We all share in that leap of faith by together reaching farther and deeper with Christ. Individuality we fall short. Together, the grace of God lifts all of us. The devil wants to divide.

Problem Events

The trust He has of us is displayed in the freedom He gives to us to act in His Spirit.

We are daily torn by the experience of circumstances upon our nature. Here is an opportunity for God.

Acting in His Spirit means allowing Him authority in our problems of life.

His love is the active force behind His incarnation in our lives.

What takes place is a certainty of faith determined by the will. We so believe in Him that His character is reconciled upon the event in consideration.

That's what it means for us to act in His will. Only a surrender of our nature to find Him at the core of the circumstances bringing about union with us can we accept and deal with these concerns.

It is when we settle with Jesus that a godly fashion emerges.

Then we can accept His peace and continue in victory with Him.

Mission

Our mission is to bring our brokenness to His healing of wholeness. We can only do this by a life of charity.

When He wills for us an exchange is set up. As we surrender, He glorifies the baggage we release. Mission lies in this glory. He reveals this to us as we follow love's change in us. No longer is all love held to priority but unconditional as well. There, we know mission, for it heals us by service.

What brings us to total union is our finding life is not what we make of it but what He does. There is what mission we have. But we may never find this until we are His immortality.

We love in this life to serve Him. He speaks by saying we are that love.

I am sure He is so pure in us that many times we oversee rather than see the work of His love. We need to be of faith for such fruit.

The Way We Walk

We walk the ways of stray cats, ever in search of home. It is a quest to alter ourselves by our fullness of life. Reaching out, we find the balance to hold spiritual and practical condition for our humanity to enter forth.

It is in stretching limits we understand how we come into balance.

A quest it is to know and hold life in a knowledge of making for excellence. It's not ours to be excellent, but the life that leads us through living. We are to have continued transformation that leads into peace and satisfaction. That is ours to surrender to a life of us in balance.

What appears as validation is ours to call a door to this fullness. It is a fullness in that delusions and ignorance are not. What is a myth is no more. We sit on truth—the truth life makes with us.

The fullness of life changes as we accept roles in new challenges and maturity. Yet it is always before us, a gem being cut with our perfection. Some say salvation. Others call it vision.

What Comes Holding Us to Time

In the space of time we are called to life, we are a passion. Our passion is in every breath and depth of life. We make effort to be a light of truth. We view every effort as a subline act of mercy on our part. Mercy for our very soul.

The very hope in life exists every day we find before us.

Here, we gather together as one flame brightly burning with precious love. Love that life's true hope hold to us.

The way we give our heart away to be loved is a clear message of how we have passed clear of the trials of each joy we know within love.

The stubborn may refuse to lose their hearts. But they will be healed.

Loving is the greatest joy we can entertain. When we speak by love, our heart knows no greater mercy. We are aware we live together What's more we see how together, there is much more than our vanity.

What we call life, it is much more than us and love seals this hope in us. The passion of our life is the freely burning flame of love.

His Light, Our Glow

The light fades. Life ebbs. As we find our heart, we notice it looks different. No longer is the vitality of a youth. Rather, our innocence has been marked by the scorings of time.

We have not the scorings timeless but rather temporal. In the moment we live, the eternal passes before us, the life of God.

As we cope with the fact that the eternal breath of God has left us, we know we are very common.

Faith pursues us to our dying. Here, God shows why we are created; when in doubt, we see our commoners.

We are our own affliction, the pride of life. But once that veil is stripped, God has His opportunity.

In Godspeed, He matches our soul with His loves.

He saves us, not on our own. Faith flies us beyond imagination to His hope for us.

The Image of Love

Love is a measure of the good we are. It shows the perfection to His Spirit and likeness we are. The use of love determines its fullness. Where it is to reach the heart/soul of one is in contrast to when it seeks the face of God inside us. When things are no longer personal but divine in desire, so love changes from mere acceptance to sacrifice in surrender. It is in how we commit ourselves to good that signifies how we commit ourselves to God.

To be in love with God means to have the same move of spirit and the same thought of love He holds. He makes love different for each of us to hold to each other so there is a difference in us and in others. Simply so we know God through the sum of people we know and not simply how one is indistinguishable from others.

The Love of His Heart Is Fulfilling Hope

The love we give is seen in how we give freely of ourselves. It is an answer we give to prepare for God.

Each day, we prepare the way for God. Hope is the fulfilling of us.

It is in that fulfilling we discover how God has made our life a blessed joy in His love.

As we move to climb the mountain of His desire in faith of Him, we discover how true is His heart. So revealing of our humanity. It is by His Spirit that His heart is formed by the love we have. It is here He says to us that we are pure as being in Him. He leads us to deeper conversion by the purity He sees in us.

It is in being a manifestation of Him we discover Him. His revealed heart in us sets us in motion to act godly. Being a manifestation of Him brings us to life that is a fulfilling of His hope.

Revealed

All we wish for is God. To be is to know God or we are an illusion.

Either we love or it is a mind game.

When we find humility, the heart breaks under the pressure of sincerity. Truth runs through us, the Holy Spirit.

God gives us reality, eternal love.

We give God authority to bring oneness to our will. It is His unity for our deepening. Our person has a deepening which is our character as determined by our experience of revelation.

The deepening of this character is the building of our faith.

In conversation, we find the means. By melding our hearts, God emerges us to truth. We become revelation.

Life Suffers Us to Love

Love enters us. Transforms. And leaves.

The Spirit of God is life to all and is a breath engendered as God's essence, love.

In life, love enters us through relationship. Only God's relationship is permanent. And only through it can we honor other relationships.

By the cross, Jesus made our relationship to Him holy. All He asks is for us to do the same to all other relations. To live out our cross means finding the love of the Spirit to allow the world to nail us.

Love enters. We are nailed. Love leaves.

It is a higher love than suffering. A higher faith.

Our victory comes not in our strength but by our Christlike nature. Nailed by our brokenness.

His Walk for Us

More often, we find God helping us up to victory. He brings us up off our knees to where He walks, giving us the peace and jo of His sovereign nature.

In the Lord, we walk amidst those past, those whom the Lord called thusly. To be in the present honoring the Lord so is to recognize how timeless His call is for us. And we are caught up in that timelessness, love.

Purer than any hope we can muster. His love draws us deeper and fuller. We embrace Him made more by love, so the ravages of the heart are quelled, and our soul is a part of His mystery.

The feelings of faith differ from those of the flesh in that one kind leads to a desire of virtues, while the other leads to carnal appetites. This is where we walk carefully, for as we enter more deeply with the Lord we enter into higher levels of give and take until our walk is Christ's selfless love.

Suffering's Perfection

The time comes for everyone to have their moment of truth. Here, they decide the nature of their will. It is a reckoning of human suffering, something we were meant for.

Each soul's suffering is an opportunity for God. It is our opportunity to show our medal.

What we pursue in our suffering is an ideal reconciliation of peace for our weakness. It is a surrender that brings healing.

I can only know from my feeling in this matter that until we remove ourselves from attachments Christ is not risen in us. And will remain on the cross until we give control over.

In the natural suffering is crying, in His kingdom suffering stretches our faith and is a deeper surrender. Suffering can be a grace for healing.

We are frail and each's suffering calls out, but only the prayer with His righteousness reaches Him. He is the God of His children. They are those who love by His love.

Willingly We Listen

We only wish for Jesus to befriend us. We need to hear Him. The words of compassion heal us.

As the trinity lives within, through, and as the life that leads we become.

The Spirit speaks revelation for us to discern His will for all life. We are formed in His image, His presence, and have His likeness, love. To be so is to have Him speak His will to us.

In being in Him and loving His will takes place. In this dynamic, revelation takes place that shows how He speaks. It is in our conscience or discerning He talks. He uses us as a vehicle for His expression.

Whenever one person of the Trinity speaks, all of God speaks. To know He speaks is to see all the character of God exposed. We work with God and so it is when He talks. He talks to form our will.

The Creator's Design

In life, God is the Creator of who we are.

If we had no struggle in life how meaningful would it be. Meaning is life's struggle to know Him.

It is a struggle bridged as we apply His seed of faith to our life.

Such a marvelous gift to make good out of who we are.

We are that quintessential clay in the Master's hands. Such creativity to bring lasting life to one so temporal.

Entering into life comes with His knowledge upon us. It means we know being human means being alone. When we are born in Christ, we are loved.

What is better than to find the fellowship of God. To be so real is our hope for life, and Jesus makes life real.

God's creativity forms life to be as we walk to Him. We are formed by His life to breathe eternity and touch glory, Him.

Healing

Because we are in His land, we learn uniquely how to suffer. It's a process of learning how to call for Him with heart and soul and to receive Him. It's a gift by our covenant nature. He calls us to godly suffering.

It means living the mystery of His crucifixion.

Learning to suffer so means how we carry our cross, together. By giving Him our brokenness, we are raised from this life.

Our love is a mercy for healing. He stores in us this love by personal revelation. Here, He excites us to joy that counters the words of our pain.

The healing of wholeness comes when we accept the word of revelation as the basis for our soul to have life. It is this that brings an unquenchable hope that holds our belief so we are in His faith. A faith that so speaks to us it is ours.

We walk with our cross to live His passion so we can transcend life.

Humility Follows God

God shows us to life by tests of faith and personal strength. Strength in combination with faith gives us the leverage to smash our bondages.

Uprooted by a negative experience we seek to establish ourselves in a fuller light of Him.

It takes the time to accept His peace to hold us to His rock of faith. The strength comes when we see Him within.

A word comes supported by love that cuts the mist upon our soul and brings a new measure of healing to what lies raw in our heart. This is how He takes us away from the tempting of the dark side's destruction. He brings His hand upon us, and at once, we are saved.

A large part of our healing is accepting the miracle that has taken place. The devil doesn't want the credit to go to God. He wants us to glorify ourselves.

Reconciling Lives

Reconciling our time of life becomes difficult when we slow-down. The imperatives are blurred and less than distinct. It is as if our vision suffers from the blended activity. What may appear distinct in the heat of a moment is not.

We call upon the Holy Spirit for grace. In our best efforts to form reality, we find limits. That is where it takes faith to overcome. Faith that God wills are only a part of revelation to be revealed through us.

As we deepen our task, it is clear we are capturing life midstream. Our revelations will only be as good as faith can bring us closer to the Maker. He shows us life, and we can take full grasp or let it go. There is no place for the hesitant.

When we do take full hold, our charge of life only gives full vision. What before was vague becomes clear. He loves us, and so there is life. It's not for interpretation but admiration. Life is for us, and we are perfect so.

Surrender

The approach of faith can be less than desirable when God is not personal or we do not let the Holy Spirit in our life.

To not have the deepest of fellowship with God is to be lacking in our surrender. To not let the Spirit of God in our life is also to be lacking in our surrender.

Faith without surrender is dead. The less of a surrender we make, the less vital is our relationship.

Surrender comes when we empty our carnal nature at the cross and pray so He makes us Christlike.

In faith, we can never do it without grace.

It defies judgment. We can only detect it by discernment. Here, the gifts of the Lord present themselves to us in faith.

Too many times, we surrender to faith and not to Jesus.

What Steals Our Nobility in Him?

The desire to be blessed is a concept of how life is a view of how divinity is a royal fashion.

What we call royal is the human nature It is divined by God and so has importance beyond our life. The royal nature of the human experience is our relationship to God.

Our experience with Him is contingent upon how pliable we are to His service. That we surrender causes us to be as clay that gains in nobility as we find service so diverse.

The disease that cripples this response is a melancholy enforced by the mediocre. It robs us of God's vision for us, and as a result of that cheapening of vision, we lose motivation.

It is not so much the destroying power of the devil we need to watch out for. It is our own pride and melancholy that is worst.

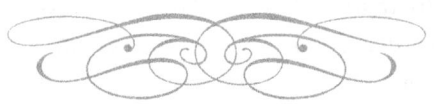

The Fullness of Life

There is an aspect to life we discount, where our responsibility lies. We think only surrender to God brings as to transparency of virtue in Him.

The more we are in concurrence with a body of Christ, the more virtue can be expected. Dogmas, teaching, all that reflects how we frame the Gospel is important.

The essential thing is to have our life as a confirmation of faith in His Life, and this begins where our relationship to Him accepts Him in faith.

We bring our relationship to His church, and there, virtue is seeded to be molded in our life.

The abiding principle to virtue in Him is to find acceptance where our heart and soul finds faith in Him. In this acceptance, we grow in faith.

God has left us with the tools to seek Him in the fullness of faith. The fullness of faith is His Life and how we approach it. This is His mystery for each of us.

Searching

The use of our time is to manifest the reality of our living in grace by cooperation.

Leading life through time experiments our valued thoughts and beliefs into faith that leads us pastime.

That life should pass us to a journey, for glory is evident in how we accept challenge for who we are.

More likely, we come to our own destiny, not knowing why.

We are a people that searches to create the place we aspire to. It is in a sense of destiny we complete things into our imperative. Only then is something personal.

What we take for reality is the limit of acceptance we have for our surroundings and our involvement with it.

It is a fact of vision limited by trust, not enhanced by faith.

So Swiftly Death Approaches

The life passes so quickly. In a moment, things change. The struggle is no more. Now the spiritual aspect reveals itself in the hiddenness now death emerges from.

The memories filled with the vitality past hold us to a course for whatever reconciliation can take place.

The moment is a filling of God's life, grace.

In love, He has sought and, in the end, finds our conclusion in Him, peace of life that transcends this life.

In this passage, time opens to the eternity within us. It passes us beyond any rivalry, failure, or desire we may have.

In our failure being not so ultimately human, godly, we discover how more in life presents us to grace upon God. He speaks a silent word. And in our silence, we understand. It is something He has held in His life for us since time in memorial, before the foundations of the earth.

Unveiling Our Reality to Further Height

A fulfillment is a workable level. In a matrix, the collection of them is a summing of ability. It is something to stretch and raise a new level of maturity. It is us finding new completion by the involvement of fulfillments. It's not in how one does, but in how one finds them in belief of hope.

The conviction of hope rescues us out of our human role to someone who makes life from love.

The whole process of recovery is to crack the shell of self-consciousness to reveal us to a more open, showing of our real nature. Not one built upon artifice but the way of the heart, to seek all creativity that prospers us to love. God is the supreme creativity, and these we are most real.

Our Reality

When we see a reality, something is high and another low to own sight. When faith is operating, reality is truth that lives for God, not for us until we empty ourselves of this world. It means we are blind and only can feel with the heart.

Reality is formed from the clay of experience either God's or ours.

In knowing recovery, salvation has got to be the paramount. If it is not lofty in us, then we are a beast of our own sweat. God makes us so that we can walk in covenant, not by our strength but by His faith. We need transparence. To allow virtue in our heart is no longer to sweat as a beast but to soar with wings of love.

To have reality is to be real for God.

His Life We Become

When I turn to God, He breathes life in me. I am so enamored. So much in love. He exists as the pleasurable oneness of my heart and soul. Beyond faith, He exists to us, supernatural and more. Beyond description. Simply all that is life.

In His mystery, we exist to embrace Him. Truth that forms us life to belong in His creativity.

Where His touch will lead is into the ecstasy of His love, Christ.

We are a blessing of His nature to find God in all of life. God is love, and to find God is to love.

Our way of life is made to serve with meaning that extends prayer. We nourish our soul in prayer. His life we become is a prayer for His fellowship.

To be set free is being born of His Spirit. That is the life we become.

The Enduring of Friends

We see how friendship ploys our very nature. It brings us to our knees. Here, the soul matches and regroups with another.

Love is the whimsy of fate. Only in enduring the friendship of another can we reconcile love to passion. It is a passionate fire to offer our hearts to the Lord's examination. It means service for God and man.

Jesus does this for us by having us enter in His passion. Our heart is cleansed, and we are made ready for enduring relationship.

The earth is alive for Christ. It responds to this hope by having people seek each other, in search of Him. He is the enigmatic face of relationship. Here He is. There He is.

Only in relations graced by the Lord does He truly exist.

Holy Life

When I come into Him, I am in the midst of love's splendor. It means I am granted to receive a grace of reality upon my soul. An intention of faith. A will that lives and gives life. It is the destiny we find in the Spirit. A love so pure it melts the incarnation through us.

It is here the grace of reality for me that I find God so evident to possess my soul and give my heart strength to live in devotion. Here, the usual ties of the Trinity draw me into His presence.

In this unison, I find impeccable joy. So divined is life. The clarity of vision develops. Openness is a sign of His hiddenness in me.

In a view of heaven, He sees us as perfect. The knowledge of Jesus. We need to hold on so perfect we are.

All Is God's

Being saved means salvation works throughout our life to place our sin nature in grace with our sins and with their just reward.

Salvation is a process of redemption or sanctification.

Recovery is a process of betterment that is a sanctification.

With salvation, there is a divine gifting for a permanent result of good.

For recovery, there is a mortal gifting for an improvement of a temporal nature.

One is redeeming. The other is improving. But they are both for one's betterments lasting and temporal.

In this way, they act as an incarnation of dual methods, divine and earthly.

God calls us to be complete in Him. Why wouldn't we want to put faith and work together for His glory.

My Light

What I need is for Christ to make me Christlike in all ways. I cannot be in harmony with others if Jesus is not with me.

To be as Christ, one needs to affirm the life He is and how we are a part of his indispensability.

Whether it is positivism or not, matters little as long as the heart of faith pulses with belief. We were not meant to languish our life but to celebrate with victory for it.

I am far from perfected in my struggle, but knowing Him, I am much further than imagination.

Where I am led is to a better place for the heart. It is Jesus, the source for my heart that brings me to know and love.

I can only be in His glory to know peace and myself.

Reality's Gateway

Most likely, we never come to our fateful conclusion. We just go on life in our many ways. Sometimes, reality arrives at our doorstep. What happens is a result of chance and faith.

If we get to know who we are, it's possible we could grow. But even that isn't necessary.

Recovery is not a choice but a statement for life.

Living a life is the way of a faceless person. When we know ourselves, recovery speaks to us.

We are formless beings waiting to be formed into a heart of the discipline that only exceptional creativity can manage. It is a creativity that binds the heart to a true and rewarding path of life, with the vigor of honesty and devotion.

A blind man may see better than a man in recovery.

We need to see how we are and are not formed. We may need some peripherals.

Love

What loves so deeply in me is the love of My Lover. He is God. He is pure. He loves beyond my distinctions. I find lovers in me by Him. He teaches love to me. I find other's love in Him. I grow so that love is complete.

He says love to know and be reality.

I love His reality, my life.

What loving does is bring Jesus alive in me. I am more Christlike.

His love is a rapture of the senses.

To love so completely is our motivating word we need to be immersed in His Spirit.

Whether life continues or ends, His love transports us to Him. In that way, we live in perpetuality.

Our wanderings of mind lead us to the dusty aspects of life where love seems questionable. Yet even here, His is the magnificence of love. He is so much more than constant but essential. Love is so only He can make it.

Coming Home

When Jesus comes to us, we are removed of hindering attachments. Our soul is freed to Him.

The more this happens, the softer our heart becomes. So soft that the Holy Spirit convicts our very being of having faith in Jesus. So assured we are elders of His faith, seeing well where unity draws all His people into His fullness.

Sometimes, even elders cannot distinguish faith from superstition, so remarkably interwoven they are. As good and evil are in this life. We cannot destroy what is of faith to get at what holds superstition. We must allow Christ to make an end-time harvest of this wheat, so we don't prematurely pull out the weeds.

Even elders need to divest themselves of their raiment of faith and enter the experience of others with simply a heart of faith. And witness how differently they carry their cross. Then one can remark on the wonderful unity in His Church.

God in Our Life

In the heat of controversy, God is silent waiting upon us for conscience. The understanding this employs is that left on our own, His gifts will shine on our humanity's will.

There is a feeling we tap in these situations, indecisiveness. This kind of anxiety dwells deep and arrives with us losing balance.

Who wants to be undermined is found by how one wants to surrender to others.

We need His input on our life. Only that direction can bring the conscience.

When God speaks, our soul rises from the ashes of this life.

Transforming comes when we are in His joy for us.

Whenever we are beside ourselves, God is patient so we can emerge into our reality. There is a time we anticipate love and don't know its passing.

Each morning offers a day, a new exchange of faith.

His Walk in Us

My Lord rises above the clouds. He sees the anchor of life in all of us. He gives us a flag to raise above misery.

Joy is His countenance as He becomes our victory. We wear His pride on our walk of faith.

We are vessels of peace to bring a balm of hope to the lives of all. He shows us peace to raise our vision, so we can see Him. In Him, we are given a hope that heals. We are set on a course that brings life.

Each day is more, blessing on blessing. We only have to depart from vanity, and the mirror will show Him, in full pleasure of us.

By the reward He shows, eternity is our home. We transcend life to broach His very mystery. When we walk with Him we have this confirmed. The Holy Spirit convicts of our love, so He is real and alive that we can say we are.

In His Joy

There is a peace beyond.

It is here He causes change, so we are His to bring into ecstasy. It is a living of His truth. This bears us to His soul.

We are special that in Him we are given reality. It is an acknowledgment of His reality in our life.

The answer to life's vicissitudes is our emptying of our self in favor of His life.

The carnal has no means by us. We are forged of the virtue of His love, a conscience universal in scope. We are entirely described to enter His word as an image of His being.

There is a hope in this quiet. Here, we see beyond the necessities of this life to the depth the eternity has worked into the time surrounding our lives.

It is a word of life.

Prophetic as private revelation, it existed to be uttered into new life.

It is the eternal joining us to Christ.

Migrations of the Mind

What transports my imagination to a mysterious reality. I am locked into a means. I lack for explanation. This day is so refined. My life bears the score marks.

So confounding. It cries an emptiness, leading me on further. In being so lavished, a grace extends me further on.

As credible as the wind, I flow with an effort unknown. The watermark of life is our creativity to form believing faith.

That we are ennobled with life is the act that we live it. The end to pursue is what He says divinely to our hearts.

This life that makes us in a making of us is without compare.

Our effort is the flight of a bird on its way, cresting and turning.

The soul seeks the light, only its falters because the heart sees the way.

Certain we are mindful of Him, we pursue living that life directs.

A means is a position of trust handed over to uncover a journey.

The Blending of Eternity

The perfection of the Lord is love. Peace is the melding of faith and reason. Love is His active influence. When we are transparent of self-sufficiency, He fills us, as each time we come before Him, we fill Him.

As in every time in Him, we are uplifted so that our souls can learn to fly; His love challenges us. It asks if we have given so freely that we grace life in His divinity.

We imagine life as a causal relationship, inspiration inspires. To see eternity in this passing is a fleeting thought. But that is how eternity works on our temporal life, as inspiration. That is how we come to know Christ, as the Source. What comes is of the loving essence, until we get to now. Grace, the action of love. That is what our wholeness in life becomes.

In the process, our soul soars in His love, simply by our contemplation of Him.

We can only live in His divinity by purging our human nature in favor of a godliness of Him.

To be so of virtue is to find a passing of death. Essential with the eternal we enter His life of inspiration.

Life's Passing

As the time of life passes, we have rarefied moments. Moments of discernment and of confusion. How we manage is by deliberate faith.

The unknown becomes ugly. So that what once was embraced loses dignity. And us with it. Change is making the unearthing of the past.

We are a viable fragment. Reduced to an incomprehension.

Grieving is our consciousness.

The nature of life makes desperate our seeking of peace. We encounter our frailty. It is a brokenness only God can love. Man cannot dignify it.

In a stupor, we find hope in the passing by saying in you it shall remain. It will drive and carry you to finality. A pained experience has become a bulwark against any more, disappointment redeemed.

A Process of His Life

The way life leads us to heavenly places, the more we will praise the Lord.

The idea of His life is to secure a real hope that lasts in our living reality. It is for the temporal of life to give way to the eternal. And thus comes the passing of us into death. It is a death that holds the supernatural door to godly freedom.

God is in answer of our hopes. He augments His life in us to a just view. He has passed a right way upon us that is in keeping with His final justice for all. Only we have come forth as His elect. Others will know only His grace and not the calling to it. Out of the depths of humanity, they will come.

The way my life leads is no different. It is conceived as a grace of God to act directly on my life and into others. It is here I find lasting and meaning in Christ. He wants me to know Him so I am love. This is redemption.

At the Core

What comes of one's efforts is dignity which calls for purpose. It is a look at the integrity, the character. That which laid hidden is revealed. Our way to express dignity is purposed.

Our heart lies within this dignity. Through our living, we seek to find that heart. Inside are all the experience of life captured by living. It is the essence of how thoughts, emotions, and faith divine in us.

It is a story of growing up and how we realize our age.

The heart meshes between the physical and spiritual. For anything to cry with life, it must have one.

God is always touching it to bring us to a newness of life. When we know this has happened, the heart has boundless love and faith. The heart is the strength of the soul.

Resurrection Thinking

What we need is an infilling. An answer to this. A way to express this life beyond time.

We have God's blessing to be. To be eternal. To be so fellowship builds.

Our goal is to grasp His creativity of us. More than we can intend is His design for us.

We think of lost opportunities to reconcile them to the present. We cannot be satisfied with the moment. We have to leverage it by the past. And then the hope for the future is muddled.

To let His design come for us, we must step to faith in the moment and not what we can do about the stigma of the past. The design will take care of that through the path to the future. In the present, we seed for the future and not for the past.

Success Planeslip

Recovery is keeping in touch with what life's reality is saying and not what fiction it thrives on.

Only then does every day become a challenge to find how one's own truth can answer that reality. Daily we must ask, what is the truth of me that answers life?

The kind of response is formed by our awareness. If we haven't been opened, it is unlikely we will freely step out of our conformance to the fiction of life.

Even still, it is not enough to step into a more real living. One must have a vision of recovery for themselves.

And this comes from knowing recovery, and what it can mean for one.

To me, it means developing an order of business that fits to my changing habits. Developing a discipline that I can grow with improvements. Learning with newer insights how life can be a friend in recovery, and not an adversary by knowing myself better.

When We Love Recovery Is Who We Are

The idea we come out of God's creativity tells us we have a creative experience engrained to the depth of our soul. This means a creative force undergirded us. We are formed so we can form.

Then comes the task of knowing recovery from life's stigma. It means having full capacity to choose life by any instrument and find how dear we become.

To do so means accepting what life has given or not so we are whole in heart and soul. We must let our abiding nature of God show us low to be creative and how to seek fulfillment. To know is to reveal our true nature. Only this is recovery.

It means we express God as love and know ourselves as we love.

Intentions: Holy and Made to Be So

What often we see is the work of injustice, as so how we perceive it. It shows how God works through us and others to cause His glory.

In us, we see how grace flows. In like fashion, He gives grace to make holy our intentions. And in doing so, we can see how as prayers of faith each runs as an obstacle for each. In a case of injustice, no one is shameless. Accusing each other as the unworthy one we all share in our own lack of mercy. God can only work through us for peace because the fitting of holiness upon our intentions is incomplete. And thus is the justice God metes out. We are our own justice.

Our hope must not be in finding God dispensing grace when we do not have the heart for it. Rather, it is in how the Holy Spirit can bring us to lament over our condition to soften our heart for His intentions. Our own intentions, however held in prayer, are of a holiness that speaks of an undelivered soul. We need His intentions to make us holy, not to glorify our thoughts and acts.

In His is union. In ours is isolation.

Living Honestly

When we face the wall of denial, how many times will we believe the same old, worn-out phrases that lock us into accepting limitations and not take the plunge to greater personal maturity and freedom.

We become locked into an iconoclastic version of what we think our virtuous self boils down to.

Each time, we go through a ritual to validate ourselves and confirm who we allow ourselves to be.

In the strict sense, a gospel life is one without the buttressing of words, because it means the heart has been so transformed that it operates automatically in the will of God.

What we need is such a change of heart that our abilities are gospel to their intention. We need to remove the mitigating notions.

It comes down to an examination that detects and confronts these notions so the face value of our life can come clean to the light of day.

God Is a First

The unblemished lamb we become. With faith enabled by Jesus Christ, we approach Him, the Father. The Spirit is with to bring a triune communion with us, within us, and through us, Emanuel, and so we abide.

It would be a time we shine our passion for the Lord. In it, we have a perfect peace driving us. And operate in a clear optimism.

We have got the beeline for help, God. He offers us unconditional love, agape, to know Him but, so He will do the best for us.

And we learn what is best for us.

We love Him.

The Perfect Will

The power of positive thinking cancels argumentative thinking over all things, once the point of view has been established.

The positives are a cure all. Greater faith invites prayer. Worship brings prayer to fruition.

Knowing just what Christ does for you is a plus, entry in the kingdom of God as a child of God and an abiding relationship with Jesus.

You have been baptized in water and fire. You have been saved.

Whatever your path to Jesus, it has been sanctified to His perfect will.

He loves you.

The Finished Work

We are the finished work of Christ. It's for us to claims our gifting, our immediacy with God. It is our healing to His Will. That is our authority.

Every strongness must be crushed. Every high thing brought down. Christ has overcome. He is the Victor. Our world, flesh, and the devil have all been defeated. He is the Victor. All in Christ share His victory.

We are a resurrection people. And the living water flows, God's abundant kingdom.

And we are the Keepers.

I love you.

In Tune with God

The helper comforts me into edification of God Almighty.

He rules the love we are by fellowship. Our faith is the strength of it.

The fulfillment of faith in God is the answering of our prayers. It is some new wholesomeness with God that is demanded, a mother view, an emptiness of the world. It would be as if the world was against you.

When you feel empty of ambition, let your prayers guide you. And no principle comes forth, sheer godliness. The power of faith takes over. He is within, about, and above.

The Promise of the Holy Spirit

Holy Spirit is the manifest glory of God through Jesus Christ. He is the old guitar player in the DVD. The three Marys are the female singers at the time of His resurrection. They all compose at the end the last chapter of the book of Revelation, the new Jerusalem. It is a passion play.

In the Pentecostal way, it is a wake-up call for believers to evangelize.

The fact of deliverance and healing through Jesus is brought to the fore. It is a Holy-Spirit-anointed worship. It plays across the finished work of Jesus.

It invites prayer tongues to be used.

Belong to God

The means God uses the Spirit is to be curious over our hearts. It makes us notice the inspiration our hearts have been teeming with grace. He is aware of our commitments and keeps us steady, so we are aware of His doings. He does not confirm His work and open the door to His emboldening of grace. We confirm it by our attitude of gratitude.

He has healed me beyond any relational pain. He concierge with the magistrate. Thank you, holy family.

Jesus in image is the man of smith. And Darlene is Mary in vogue. Music is faith.

All in worship of God. Holy Spirit headship.

Our Walk with Him

God has done it all. We just walk in His footsteps. Just keep with the Miracle Spirit. That presents God's favor.

In faith, we find that God has a storied place for us.

In the healing of our heart, He calls us to believe.

As we believe in faith for our victory with Christ, we are love it takes shape. Redeeming the present unto healing of the past. We look to His healing to guide us. Out of our flawed behavior, into the fruit of the Spirit and praising God for their victory, yours and His emerging.

God is here with the godly abiding well with Him.

Alive and Authentic

We are called to His kingdom. We are of the light. His very nature resonates with us.

He is our certain hope. We know Him by His presence.

Thank You, Holy Spirit.

We are community. Blessed and free in Him.

God sets life and death before man. Choose life.

He is our Light. So in Him shines the one who sent Him.

Abba, thank you, Father. Thank You for Your hedge of protection.

Graced

As I wonder about this community, I see Him in many splendored ways. These are His children. Godly men and women. All bring gifts of their past to glorify His name.

They are walking their faith to God. He has His eyes on every soul. Godly they remain in His kingdom.

We share a goblet of His righteousness. The cup runs over with faith. God has mercy. We know each other through His eyes of faith, love, and hope.

His Love Endures Forever

Although I tire, I will not tire for the Lord.

The Lord wishes peace among His kindred. The abuse of given names must end for the true names to be respected.

People are seen as gifts through God's eyes. Do not spoil that which God is pleased with.

We all make errors of judgment. But God corrects all with love.

My errors bespeak of my flaws. God knows I love imperfectly.

He Is My Master

Whatever God gives we are blind to is a bonus. Jesus is a Giver of life. We surrender as according to Your desires. We just don't give ourselves carte blanche according to our will. We give ourselves over to You according to Your will. We surrender to You.

You have a higher calling, according to Your will, for us.

To love as God is Agape. For us to be Agape is accepting His image.

In gasps, I render myself.

I am not Christ but an image. Imaging His Love is all I am. I give away as according to the Spirit.

In the Firmament of Heaven

The magisterium in its high communion of Trinity and Holy Host is incomparable with agape love for all.

This communion always rests in us. The agape love stirs us to untold limits. Praise God.

It is a perpetuating ardor of love that pests right the relations of mankind. To just believe in Him is a hysteric high grace.

We were born to love and to share it, totally. Your destiny is right before you. Enkindle the flame in your heart to a roar Christocentric in love's graces.

The Lord is particular how He shines agape, to meld us and Him.

Capitol or Blessed

God has lasting grace for those who find Him in their every day. His blessings are a fitness for life at any level, a heart to know His perfect love and inventiveness to find inspiration to make equality of blessings a call for individual creativeness an answer to capital inequality, love shared and given.

To be freed of curses of wealth is to be born simply. Extravagance invites excess of pride and comparisons. Shame, blame, and guilt are enough to deal with in the natural.

Simply born is an excuse for humility. Born for wealth is no excuse.

Pride, Capital Lose, and Gain of Ego

The serenity of agape love in one's heart signals that it is ready to come forth. In the proper order of grace, it will or be our hose.

It comes forth as we bring other anticipations to our reckoning.

We see how comparisons bring great loss to capitalization equality. It is better to give than to receive. In this abundant life, we share off what God has given us as excess to live with. Peace is a good standard. Love thanks the Maker equal right to benefits God gives, inventiveness and inspiration. The means for joy at any level. Not the greed of capitalization, which is a false pride. Not a humility before God, which is a love to Him for His giving nature. To walk with God is to realize what all is God given.

Love that Overcomes

When a love loses out, it's the same. What was meant to occur did.

It's like fortune mixed with liars. Too much pride.

This means what was meant for love was idolized (bias becoming racist). And it can happen if you blunt off the incoming grace (working at it with minor mercy).

Don't let yourself be caught up in the beauty of the person. Be taken by the beauty of Christ within, pure grace.

The beauty of the moment is the treat of unaccounted grace leading to Love Agape!

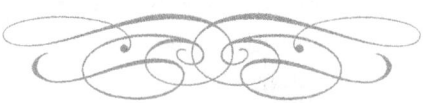

Love Never Quits

Grace upon grace is what agape is. Lover to lover.

The shear exposure to the face of love, a child, endears one.

The happening of first inspiration is clear from the heart. Think of love agape, then all becomes as in Him.

All activity becomes as graced in love. In Him, it is agape.

It is pure hope in agape. We have full faith. Our love keenly knows the Maker.

The letdown of love is us seeing through love, not being in rapture, love.

There is a clear purpose in being let down. So we seek the Maker afresh with agape.

Grace Moves

Children are major love, not to say it didn't exist beforehand.

It is a fresh recourse. God breathes love on us and a child is born. The magisterium of Christ shines upon us in the little face.

Thank You, Jesus. Yes, He is omnipotent and eternal.

From one line with Jesus, the world is saved. He is born. In one moment, we are born again. His birth is prophecy realized, a walking incarnation of God and of man, hutzpah, praise God.

We are a people of God, declared or not. God likes God.

Humble and grace led, His people.

I belong to You. Lift Jesus higher. Think before God how you are blessed. You think and can move air.

Just like God

To tap into the whole of Christ in someone is to say all that you see of them is total grace.

It is the love casting its light on your heat.

You see it every day in the people whom you meet.

It's in the music of joy. The heart sings.

The jazzy catchy music blends for loving.

The more forgiving we are of the wounds of the body, the better off we see; that includes for giving ourselves of the hard attitudes we carry. That includes our God. He does the same.

Never-Ending Love

Love never peeves away. God touches those in love. It is imbedded inside.

In the Wise, it is Him singing to us. God is able. Say to the Lord, please share your heart. He is alive in us. I'm sure He is here.

He is imbedded in grace. Christ is in each cheer. You give us free to life.

The means for grace to work is opening the heart to worship.

The workings of grace is His ability to reach us.

The HS is marked in us by the way of the conscience in us of imbedded love, where we have been like Him.

What Is the End of This?

Death is life sealed by God. Our prior time or predestination is where we meet Him in the natural.

Beyond death, life is supernatural and still we are divinely blessed.

Death is an unformidable task. It involves cessation of all we know through living. But life goes on. We truly do not know what amounts to life in this living or dying, take your pick. In life, there is a just Living. Or a permanent dying, death. Living this life and the next life is a matter of His faith and our faith connecting. In other words, death is a door from faith to faith. Or a door from no faith to permanent death.

Experience Worship

Angelic battle is counterfeit evil. The mark of God is light. The darkness needs our light to accept darkened truth, graceless truth. It is a dark hole upon all called life, the message of the magisterium.

Evil counterfiets the divine supernaturally against prayer.

The counter to evil is standing in faith of Lord Jesus Christ.

When we worship the Triune One, we accept the Gospel of Light.

We are in the magisterium. He breathes upon us the words of life.

He centers each of us.

We breathe life, the tongues of love.

Called to a Seating

The communion of the Lord is the seating at the banquet table of the Lamb.

It is the quiet resolution of our present call. It will remain so until we further gain into the five-fold ministries and the seven sacraments. Any special consecration may be a past of our seat. It is a lifetime pursuit.

The communion of the Lord is blasphemy to break it. Your seating may change but not your communion. It is your covenant.

Gifting comes with the intimacy the healing of Jesus provides. The seat is your concept of the mercy seat of Christ for you.

The Completed Work of Jesus

To all father figures I may have tripped up. My discernment will always act up. My second-guessing always does me in.

God is here in His faithful love is honor, respect, and submission.

The spiritual and mystical Church is the aim of our wedding feast with the Lamb. Union with God.

My mind goes through many contortions of decision-making with old friends. Newer friends partake of the mystical church of the Lamb with set friends there too.

The eccentric flaws I manage are my waywardness with my flesh. You must excuse my waywardness. I know salvation has more redemption to do on me. In my niche, I am fully redeemed, but my physical has a wage to go to catch up with my spiritual.

Faith's Progress with the Lamb

The recourse of faith believing is abiding well. And He is abiding well, so life may continue in Him, infinitely.

We continue in this blessing of life, looking forward to our life immortal with our Master Lord Jesus Christ, the removal of older habits heads one to opportunities otherwise hidden Christ is upon us. Thank You, Jesus. We are swallowed up in the love of God. It is a beautiful experience.

On the ledger of life, our name grown weary.
Our newer one comes through our faith in
Jesus Christ.
On the throes of Love with our great Savior and
Lord Jesus Christ.
Our only mistake is not to carry Him everywhere.

Humility Becomes Myself Alone

To catch the grace of God, one needs to be honest and detached.
Forever on immediate cares even discernment.
Be open to His Spirit activity. Peace is one in back with inspiring tones.
Each man or woman emits a size of glory to be brought up with the Spirit, Comforter/Truth be He.
Measure the rhythm and concordant activity.
It is He right here.
Thank You.
God Almighty Jesus.
All over reality worship.

The Book

I am really peeping out. Today, I received two accolades. Awesome is the task of defining Him, the Good. He abides well in me. And I within Him. The Lord God is the Lamb. God is Almighty Jesus Christ. My Lord is Jesus Christ. He is the father Yahweh. The Spirit of God keeps me.

To hate is the process of salvation, not Him; troubling ourselves may be hateful of me but not of Him. Being contrite and broken is what we are before Him, always missing something, Him.

I Am is Him. I am is me. A perfect match. Heavenly sent.

Winsome

As my time for living ebbs away, I am struck to the view, all happens for His glory. And that I grow so slow.

The radical politics is anger for any reason. I realize the conservative cause has been hijacked. And what was errors prone for me the Lord has answered by light. And what was a hope for has been a gift in realizing Him.

He lets me wander until I recognize the better of two choices.

Christocentric seems the perfect adequacy.

My rapport is useless. I find dead ends to fascinate over. Life is flirtatious. Appeal wanders. Healing is stability.

Jesus You Have Awesome the World

The Lamb of God saves us from countless language misery and hurts. He brings us overcoming power by the name of Jesus.

He overcome every temptation that would lead to sin.

It is the power and authority of His name that provides so much for the believer as resources to took his day to day and moment to moment because sincere and freedom in choice to continue in His will.

The average believer has no much regard for a call to religious holiness on his past. Maintaining one's relationship to honor God is, at most, the best from a believer.

I need the Spirit of truth and order for my maintenance. His countenance or presence be it so lands me His gravity.

A Witness

Time flies in orbs around our consciousness, the firmament of God pronounced for a vision or call. He presents Himself to truth. Hope is our engineer to complete oneness with love.

Determined to be love fulfilled we seek Christ, the Person of Love Divine. Jesus is who we are to Him. Never alike but called.

Our call is the sweetness of vinegar. It is a language overhead to what has been too far long empty in us.

The means of a call is practical ambition.

I have been taken in Him to answer my call. To be what art is to the eye, with a pen and words, encourage the light.

Living a Healing Gospel

The firmament of heaven is the constitution of faith from believers. Ever and away, the walkway of God. It points to the infinite eternity of the universe of God, the Eternal Father.

The magisterium is all the glory to God on High. God on High is Him and all His inheritance. We are His, always and forever in covenant. The strength of belief, what is of contemplative prayer.

Eternal life with God. It echoes all our hope in Him. Always healing from our humanity to our called nature, the transformative Gospel.

Jesus the Christ

The Holy Spirit of God was always hidden in the Christ of God, which simply received the full authority of God Himself when Jesus was crowned the Christ in heaven. And immediately, the Jesus Christ was most as means Holy Spirit to guide men and women. All power rests in Jesus Christ. Only in Him can we do all things. God's face now is of Jesus and He is Jesus Christ. And the inspiration of God, the Christ, now is the Holy Spirit of Jesus Christ. The Trinity now is Jesus, Jesus Christ, and the Holy Spirit of the Christ. Jesus Christ is the summation of all as God

All by Way of Jesus Christ, Yeshua

It is our inheritance of righteousness by belief in Jesus as the firmament of the Godhead through the Christ of Jesus. We are Christians. The role of the Father is, like Mary, to point to Jesus by way of the newly designated Spirit of God. At once, now, the Trinity is all faith in the Father and man pointing to Jesus, all faith in Jesus Christ, and all faith through the new covenant spirit of God, the Holy Spirit of Jesus Christ in our lives. Him in action in one is the firmament of God. He is God to us within a living relationship.

A Newer Spirit of God

The firmament of the magisterium is Christ in action through me. It was when all faith is directed to God first. Than the sufferings play a role in a match for our Redemption through Jesus Christ. Jesus only become our God by the love He had for Him, no longer in keeping the Godhead by Jehovah, but instead the Godhead through the faith in Jesus for the Godhead. The Trinity was reshaped by the fullness of Christ in Jesus. Jesus Christ summed the Godhead of Jesus by His inheritance of the Father's Godhead, Jesus now.

The Firmament of Christ, Himself

As we grope in time to manage our affairs, we count the morals of sin, powerless before the cross. We are so sinful we cannot see the cross that saved Jesus. Poor martyr. He was for our sake, He had to save Himself by the single deepest faith He had in the Father. Truly, He become God, saving Himself, and we before the impotent Father and Spirit figure He knew through prayer.

When we come into Christ's firmament of prayer, we find the Godhead of the Trinity working with us.

Thanks to God

The meaning of fulfilling our salvation akin to loss, we find ourselves trusting its answer—love.

The unity of the HS is the question we answer as we come to Christ with as without grace to Him.

If we are in Him, His grace follows. If we are simply reaching out, He will find favor for us. If we are consumed by a vice, we need to empty ourselves for the HS.

Praying to God is ineffective if we are no longer acting in and through His will. Jesus is the one who completes our prayers.

Then

The air I breathe is not but a reaction to the presence of God.
He is a while and not, a whimsical companion.
He celebrates the Lord.
Exclaiming will by the power of God through His choice of interment, till it tires into discernment.

I tire to amplification. A reckless dissertation.
I get a fullness of exhibition to the music.
Words press for meaning. Nowhere.
I look to see for motivation. Nothing.

Now

The course of grace is so inimitable. So it has a good following.
The severity of its footing is always at question.
The essential to all of this is the background of a "Life in the Spirit Seminar" series.
The Lord speaks. The Spirit invites.
He asks, "Who are you in love with?" And the Spirit invites me to say, "The Lord God Almighty." And my spirit says, "You."
Free past fear. Love that has now equal.
Whoever gets there first. It makes no difference. Each gets a relationship with God.
You wear the Victor's crown.

My Hope Is to Be Present Always

The lasting qualification for this to happen is, how close to Him are you?

Look at your life. Have you been protected? When you surrender, how do you know you mean it?

How constant in prayer are you?

Are you sure you pray?

My gasp of air is to compose His presence.

Flesh Untamed

The economic sweetness preferably relates to inclusive to gospel points of denomination. Evangelical must be muted to politics.

When the presence of God is understood, then religious nature is balanced.

To understand is to see God always working in presence with us. It is ours and His.

Around us are circumstances He uses for sin to determine better our relationship.

I gasp and one conformance to His presence heals me.

I see a holiness in conflict.

One makes justice in the mind.

The heaven of His presence in this called beauty and love of His person.

The social justice of the Libertarian is inviting with our Conservatives, hue. That is the remnant of the optimism.

The beauty of His presence is in more than me, grasp of air. It is Him breathing through us, a communion of saints.

You have to suggest newer approaches to work up concern. Thus, the politics of runners take place. The newer approaches must be social justice with a flavor of economic sweetness. Trump oversee this but kept up some principles for religious Conservatives.

Ho-Hum Views

Ambition makes one go deeper in the Lord.
Humility is all, a broken and contrite heart will do.
Faithful is a true justification (past loves of the heart).
All that we are, friends.

The Active HS

Your presence is heaven, and You declare to me in so many ways the activity of the Holy Spirit.

The Holy Spirit may be in maturity of way, too—a tingling in my head, a light in my eye, or percussion best of my body. Your presence is very involved with my person. It is the crowning of the Victor.

The matching with worship music is evidence of this activity.

From the onset, worship sounds bring the heart and mind into play. The soul dances to the Lord. Peace, love, and joy.

What Is the Passion for Us?

The call for holiness is approaching Him with celebration to blot out whatever be dark in our lives. It is Him in faith magnified to put His Life squarely in front of us, so we attend Him and not some caustic lie of the devil. We find Jesus Christ more attractive than the disappointing, empty darkness. We were and always meant for what irrigates full blessed life, and not something questioning our living. We were meant for the abundant life, the victorious life, the overcoming life of Jesus. These are everlasting words of His life. The light of His life, we celebrate in darkness.

The Passion of Jesus Trouble

The life of the Holy Spirit in one can be seen as something needing good viewing when we see there dark moments. Our heart show reminds us of Jesus, or the chaos is within. Concentrate on Jesus. Put the gifting of the HS in our heart by having the heart remind us of Jesus's passion. Choose to follow Jesus to the cross. These chaos ends, and the dark is merely a lead choice, not viewing Him on the cross, saying, "It is finished." All end dark is now seen as a lie; we can choose away from with Jesus entombed, then resurrected.

Dragging One Foot

In secret, we play and pray, not quite knowing what will happen.

I know in faith, I am tied, and know all grace comes from Jesus. As you have said, You were always caring for me. You laid the platform to inspire love. So I must lift Jesus even higher than that platform. Only with Him is that possible.

So daily I come to Him to surrender myself.

I have a couple human maid of irons in the fire, two, related began unfortunately linking of comment. I live down each day.

They are father and son. As long as they see me in Christ, it's okay.

Of Him

He reaches us when we have extended our best, not knowing Him any better.

And yet abiding, so it is better than knowing.

As it is with the unseen, there is no unknown involvement. Intimacy is not the question, compatibility is. Oneness is the issue, to love one another as He has loved us.

Death has been done away with; freedom is assured. I think of the mercy You have for us, the cross, the power of God.

Evil abounds, but grace even more so. My walk is victorious, abundant.

In Grace

He asks for us to live worthwhile in Him. We answer Him, that is enough.

We are broken in Christ-sized pieces for Jesus to enter.

To bear witness of Him is to already wait on the Holy Spirit.

Grace is the economy of God.

You have overcome, the kingdom of God is at hand. The Holy Spirit is complete within me.

My Lord Jesus Christ calls to the very deepest part of me. The Holy Spirit encourages me. As I see, the vertical payment will not be alms but done over.

Sons or Daughters, the Same

"But seek ye first God and His Kingdom and all things will be added unto ye."

The charismatic message of life, He is in us, and we are in Him.

As you believe, so you are made, a living faith. You are to Him what life is to you. The Christ child you have become. Clear of sin, anew in God to purpose Jesus in all believers. Overcoming paradise of the kingdom.

The little you are gained, the more I have become in paradise. I am to Jesus what Christ is to Jesus.

We are emblems of Christ.

Kingdom Walking

A worship experience means your whole body and soul are actively moved. You are in the control of the Holy Spirit.

It is recognition of His kingdom you occupy by faith.

No more doubts, total forgiveness. We overcome and are part of the abundancy of God.

We desire repentance and godly ways. A closer, more intimate walk. We seek God and His kingdom.

Unknown to us is how well our lives are a living penance for Him, a living sacrifice.

We walk a Gospel walk in His steps.

His Contact

The indigenous response of man to God is inherent to the naked inequity involved.

A clear response to forgiveness is clear for each response.

Whether He makes us familiar to Him is not relevant. What is clear is how we are obedient, as He makes clear His will and how we have raised at it.

He will let us sign our agreement.

It can be exuberating trying to figure how He is reading out to us.

Once agreed to, then we can continue with grace-filled moments.

He is an enabler of our graces.

Now And

Jesus is alive and well.
Authentic faith.
Is a breeze in an uncertain world.
Now the breeze multiplies.
The Father shines past us.
Holy Spirit radiates grace.
Jesus Christ is our friend.
The Son brings life abundant.
The joy of His presence.
Questions answer themselves.
He is a fire, aflame for the Lord God Almighty.
I am His instrument.

Yeshua

As we correlate with You, Your divine nature always goes beyond.
The anointing on Jesus, making Christ into Him is fantastic.
Beyond our expectations.
He is an Almighty God.
By the choice of His will, we have sonship, overcoming spirits, worshipping hearts and souls.
I find the natural regard of Your believers anointing and holy.
We belong…to Him.
Yahweh, of all names, is Him, Jesus Christ.

Beginnings

Glory, peace, love, and wonder are how we hold Him in our heart.

He is God, the Almighty. God so loves His child son. He is beyond words and yet so close. Abba, You are so incredible. You raise us from the dust to be with You always. You set the terms of everlasting life, love.

With love, You cast us in wonder about You.

We receive any and all gifting due us as we bless your name and declare You are a Holy God.

Wonder of wonders, we can only imagine how all came.

Godly Love

To be at peace with God is to have faith in Jesus for His righteousness before God.

That is being born again.

Only that is our beginning. Love for the father is next after a consuming love for Jesus, following all that for a further consummation with the Holy Spirit.

Following total love for God is one for neighbor and, finally, for oneself.

Being changed from being at peace to love is gifted. Oneness follows.

Total union with God and people is agape Love.

Love Contemplated

Be a candle of flame. Do not quench it. The passion of Jesus is what the Holy Spirit is leading us to.

For the body to be empty is that the spirit of us has left it before death to enter heaven, as the soul remains lifeless awaiting the Rapture. It will be called by the presence of God. Love continues and does not die out.

Until the hearts of Jesus move to God, then it will be matched by the Holy Spirit.

The unction of delivering prophecy is translated into finer discernment of the heavenlies, and the creative peace of the Lord now is love.

Oneness of Union

Holiness is more pertinent as the Holy Spirit is.

Oneness is our answer to His call. It means lining up in will and purpose with the loving faith of joy, so hope is secure. Then we are heart to heart with Jesus Christ if we follow. His commandments, He will love us; Yes, pleasing the Lord is always a pleasure. That is our living sacrifice to a living God.

And in oneness above all even are in Him as He is in them. Matching each other is Christocentric living, Gospel living.

And yet we have not yet arrived. That won't be until we are in eternity with the Christ.

Peace or Love

The journey from confirmation to charismatic is noting peace to love me as the basis for faith.

To exemplify, this is acknowledging the HS in one to acknowledging His leaderships.

To see what He says, "Be perfect as your heavenly father is." And, "Love and have loved you," and "I loved you first," signify a special agape coming out of love and faith, and not needy righteous faith.

The throne of the heart of Jesus and I are one.

Love as He Has

Yes, we are within Him. All faith is at hand. God is listening.

We are naive to His encounter. It is beyond our nature He arrives. In His Divinity, He comes to match our humanity in Jesus to see the Christ through us. Perfection is proceeded by Creator to creation. Perfection is a matchless process of eternalizing a human. Graces abound as we are sourced for grace. We become Christocentric, eternally.

It is the born-again journey that recognizes love on the prime ingredient in any relationship. It is the merit we receive when we put our faith in God.

Fill in Up

Our life has a call on it; we can tell by the love given it. We are inspired by it. His heavy presence, and its moments of concentration and inference.

The nature of a call is to weigh more emptying of our soul in some direction.

We need to stop our emptying by wisdom the HS supplies.

The wisdom of the HS is the recollection of the naming of God Almighty through Jesus Christ.

That takes us to the filling of the Holy Spirit.

Grace Relating to Us

Music sets the soul free. The Holy Spirit is set into motion, heart sense. We have a choice to make. Heart sense is faith and well-being to decide on the nature of sound to nourish one. We are endeavoring to deepen our relationship with God. His force being is highlighted through musical sound. We call this His living presence. It is attuned to our senses. That is how grace come to us. Emotions like reason can occur with our senses. Only that grace-led moments come in praise and worship when we elevate our relationships.

Miracles

Pick one of Jesus's miracles. Look at Jesus. He makes Himself available. Do the same for Him.

Look at the public official and his ailing daughter.

Look at the five thousand men fed with fish and bread.

Look at the wedding and the fine wine.

Look at the alien woman and her issue of blood.

Look at Him on the cross, saying, "It is finished."

Do you feel whole inside? No teeming of darkness, just good thoughts. He is with you. Be like Mary and listen to Him and read the Gospel miracles.

Set Free

The chaos, dark, in our lives is settled by following His passion. It heals us of making bad choices, separating us from His wisdom. Without the discernment of the HS, the words of Jesus make no sense. Then you need to open your person to Him and regain the mind of Christ. Then, darkness is no more, but a path to a closer walk with Jesus comes at once. Then humbly walk closer in Jesus. This is the out from the stigma of the chaotic darkness. Keep your mind on Jesus and on His words. Now hassled, look back and see the error you missed. Continue reading that Gospel and make a note of what Jesus healed you of.

Worship Jesus or give Him thanks. You have experienced some of His everlasting words of life. God bless.

The Gateway to God

The healing of memories requires an acknowledgment of Jesus—that He is the one to keep in mind with all memories. Celebrate with Christ being there. Worship so that time becomes transformative, an altar for faith and belief in God.

We give man all to Him. Then is no one like You, Jesus.

Receive Him well!

Don't accept the lies of the evil one.

Each time a bad thing occurs, Jesus can change it with faith; in Him, not in the devil, and not in ourselves. In Him.

Overcoming Dark Memories

What is meant for us is Christ. To be more in line with Jesus is to know He is life, meant to be by adaption and belonging. The evil we face is not meant for us. So we must observe ourselves from it and say it was never meant to purpose of as having life in Jesus. So we take one step closer to Him and His everlasting words of life, even if it means the resurrection for some soul in heaven. He's the only source to God the Father at those utensils. Life is the spectacle of Him in our lives, celebrating His.

Keeping with God

When we catch up to Jesus, it's only a matter of mealtime, nor have much for salvation _____ become lost at ourselves.

In this retirement place was all there is to it with the same grace to salvation. Or we can have them in its process for salvation.

Forgiveness and confession keep my trust in God. We wish exiling precious graces of love or never learn the betterment of salvation has in store for us.

We simply short shrift those essentials.

Peace in His presence is vital.

Taking Good Looks at Our Reality

You are on top of everything. You give first light to all things. You key things, so You are the same beginning to end. We work out the miserable in between. At the light, we first take advantage of You. You are coupled up with graces and mercifully have an awakening.

The fruit we wish for is the same regardless of our point of entry. Only the application of those years become more stretched. The more we delay and do not trust, we intermediate badge witness. We have to trait. It all figures the same only more and more legally strangled the more we delay and do not abide with the witness. Where there is none, we have to decide gracefully.

Teaching Family Needs

For the Lord is great, a receptacle of grace for all life. He is the source and parenthood for all of mankind. We exercise this loving Father in His grace to enlighten us and strengthen us for the journey. Each day is anew; it is a salvation for us. We are grateful people. We have chosen to walk with You and adhere to the eternal made; You decide repose.

Thank You, ever living eternal Savior of grace and honor. It is always Your teaching our family that shines on us best, always.

Never

Music is so compelling to the words and activity. Peace when it would have been glorious.

>Take the
>Wound and
>All…
>Open us.
>Pour out Your kingdom.
>God is holy. God is faithful.

Darlene is correct. We keep declaring the finished work of Jesus.

We will never be the same.

Crucified, Dead, and Risen

It's easy to put aside past wonders and current ones for the DVD. I am blessed deeply. This DVD, like Joe said, "Is all we are about." He died, but the memory of him and others is caught up in the playing of Darlene. Even the current ones. It is "a journey of God."

Jesus, You have overcome today. Te Deum!

The mistakes of the past are confessed and sanctified. Praise God.

I am Yours forever…
No one can compare to You, Jesus.
Behold the Lamb of God

You are blessed to be in His salvation.

Abiding

The spiritual is like the width to the physical. The natural is the combination of both. The spiritual is the depth love.
It is, "Go ethnos."
The more depth, the more we literally are in the hands of the Maker, Jesus Christ.
The more depth, He is with us by some sign of His. It may be of a shadowing nature our conscience takes or a sense of nudge or of something more profound. He is. Whatever the connection, if it works, He will abide so with us if we maintain so.

Time in the Shadows, Not as Abiding Life

God is always pushing past the darkness to us. He sees us, but we cannot. Faith so strong but little illumines Him to us. It is the shadow of death we occupy ourselves with. We see in the finite abstract of time. We count each day—past, present, and future, in days. The reality of faith does not reach us, only our finite nature in time. Certainly, we are in the victorious kingdom, but the absolute truth of it passes by us when we count out the time we hold in days, not as a continuum of abiding.

Gospel Poetry Afresh

Being in constant prayer means one's spirit life is well enough to act and independently of the physical nature. The natural self is now surrounded to Jesus. The image of Him is complete in nature. The healing now copes to bring the light of faith's continuum into constant prayer. Then and only then is one arriving enter with glee with the Master. The shadow of death is gone.

The light of His day presides in the victorious kingdom of Jesus. Now we talk to Him.

The Staffing of a Compromised Will

I am sure the natural and spiritual marriages make a difference. If one has both, then one is complete. Otherwise, spiritual marriage alone is like being just a convert with no temporal marriage. Totally dedicated to Christ alone. It is grace upon grace, not grace upon strife. One is responsible to a difficult level, not an absolute surrender. With the natural one as well, one can be stirred more against one's will; otherwise, one is centered on His will absolutely. There is no compromise, only surrender. In compromise comes a newer different tone.

Gospel Living

The roleplay You take us through is the presence of You, all thanks to the person of Jesus in our lives. The wholeness of Christ is upon us. His relationship is pure grace.

Salvation is Him every day. While I mull over the fate of faith, it shines on.

Faith is inseparable from God and man. It is His remarked presence. He is here as man. That is faith working among us. And we ask for it to lead us. It is a combination theory. It needs to be first to act so. So the living of Gospels postulate must be a finite. It means accepting the Word, then bringing it up by our application. Time over time, it is applied, till a living presence it is, worship. The musical lyrics we sing. The words are a play upon the personable Lord, Jesus.

God Is Here, in His Faithful

Living relationships must be tended or they go into obscurity. That means the same transparency of heart must grow within or fail. Just like faith in Christ needs constant adjusting. It is entering into an eternity.

The music of our heart guides us with its life, exuding beat of freshened blood. Our very being of heart sings a song of joy to enhance the Gospel. It is a desire to fully worship Jesus for the new graces He gives us every day. It is a rhapsody of the postulates of the Gospel; are hold so dearly. We never will be the same, as our searching goes.

Contacting Jesus

With no stretch of imagination, the HS has been cleansing me of dark might. I am better to join Him in oneness. But a far stretch to go. He is imminent and far. I am in His kingdom but feel nowhere different. I am but not, I know Him, because my heart is confused. Did I just pass through some growing or remind myself that the past has no hold on me? I am a creature of today. He was of today, so I can have confidence in Him, and I know Him by His sufferings.

Our Faith in His Presence

We celebrate our union with the HS each time we play music comforting to the soul. The presence of God invites us and celebrates our union and draws us closer to God, His presence.

Less of me, more of Him is how eternity forms for us. We are not annihilated, but there is an immeasurable amount of Him to our finite self. Yet the strength of graces works in our favor. So holy is our union, ever centered on Jesus, the Son of God. We are so face that we want to worship God.

The presence of God underlines our faith in Him.

The Physical Presence

Happy He finds us we all are brothers.
To feel His embrace is the activity of HS in us.
When we say, "Abba Sweet Jesus," He is upon us.

Our soul knows the call of God. It passes through death to Him when our body dies. With our heart in Him, God Almighty, we are complete in Him, eternally.

You have me divinely. I love you with all my grace, superior You are. Time passes by eternity, time and time again, You.

Abba Answers for the Holy Spirit

His passion answers all questions. If even we have a human question, compassion is His answer—selfless, compassionate, and graced love. Within the Spirit of truth, the Comforter, the Holy Spirit, all of this is possible once we admit to sinning, arousing upset in another. Good motives might not be enough if we are not empathic in our initial action.

Worship will start the right answer. Contemplative quiet will finish it.

Contemplative quiet will answer the question or indicate if more time is needed.

A prayerfulness is a good repose to take, resting in the Spirit.

Ask God if it is enough, Abba.

The Creative Peace of Jesus

Enlightenment spells inspired truth God has for us when in a quarry. It reflects the gifts of the Spirit active in us. It is a spiritual answer for any time-ridden question.

It brings God alive to His presence with us. We can detect the mind of Christ by imbibed inspirations. We have rested in the Lord sufficiently for Him to speak in the quiet.

Peace is God's element in the quiet He uses to talk with us. It is inspired enlightenment we now carry the spirit of to reach an inspired quiet of His peace answer. Some call it the work of prayer. It is the Holy Spirit.

Enlightenment Is Truth by His Graces

God Almighty looks at His kingdom and rears within at the godly men and women. Holy creatures in His image. They are Holy Spirit lives.

Gifted they are, they have never forgotten the Giver.

The justice of God lies in their bosom.

We follow His presence. Only then we are in touch with the selflessness of His prayers for us, for it is sheer graciousness. Where we become holy unto Him is our point of contact, and He answers in new graces of appreciation of His life, inspiration.

Your Family

And we think we are set free to anything. Just as being holy means being separated from all sin, being free means now we can worship God, meaning we have relationship. Covenant ties cost to God Jesus is our all within all.

All reminds us of the beauty of truth. Jesus keeps us that way.

The family of God is always ready to your need. They are the ones who share and bear love.

For these there that the Holy Spirit has allowed to touch you.

Living Whole

The love of a selfless man frees us of sin and whole. With a Christianized kingdom language, I proceed to my writing.

Alone with paper and pen and begin. Thinking of Him comes first, then many papers.

I had experienced salvation with a fervor of faith.

Now I gleam the blessedness of communal life.

I use music or TV as a backdrop to prayers, worship, healing, or reading in my solitude.

Give Christ Your Last

The Lord says to me, "Overcome your world, the flesh, and the devil." "I have come to give you life and overcome your fears." "Give your last to Christ and live."

It is a call for holiness I have in this place. That means blessing others. My desert experience has given me self-control. So the flesh is manageable. The world is my lasting obstacle to keep me humble for Him.

Influences of the devil are negated by the name of Jesus. In writing, I wait on the Holy Spirit. When Jesus is, clearly is heard, I write my overflow of Jesus. He is patient.

To the Triune Love Peter

The tool of writing is to determine what process to holiness is more effective.

Whether it be focusing on the movements of the Triune God or on one Person specifically I write.

Relations to the Godhead are multifarious, meaning that for different reasons, we tap into the varied nature of Him for different degrees of holiness and reverence.

Reverence and holiness, we can offer ourselves to God through our relationships; we can make love letters.

He Is Our Savior and Lord

He teaches me to be a living sacrifice for Him and mankind. My grace is His. He is gracious. That is His salvation, us. We are His graciousness on the cross. What the cross is a means to live out His sacrifice while in holiness we offer such, the sacrifice of faithfulness of relationship to the One Holy God of three persons. We are triune in our satisfaction of Him.

He teaches that His cross, we all are born to be His children, by love, ascending in all graciousness. To find His healing touch.

My Cross Is Because He Teaches Me

Your Pleasure is mine to bring to You. Your pleasure pleasures me, pleasuring as well. Truth, by Jesus His Son, is the greatest pleasure. Truth, by the Triune relation, is great as well. Truth, by the Spirit of truth, is great as well.

To please the Lord God Almighty is my greatest pleasure. The faithfulness I bear for Him is my greatest pleasure, my holiness of relation.

The good in my relation is His pleasuring me. Yes, He is God, only He. That makes it holy for me as well.

Your overcoming is perpetually with me as I see You on the cross. I see my heart and His.

Close Your Eyes to See the Kingdom Here

You broke the hold of the devil, death, and the graves at the cross.

All were set free as He is to the call of holiness with the Triune One, God Himself, Father, Son and Spirit. A Holy Spirit believer.

Consumed in heavenly grace, we are one with Him.

Perception is a keen notice of the obvious. We can only see at the natural level, whereas the spiritual victory has got to be in the mystery of faith. There we are in the kingdom.

Bless Us Again

Are we just fools in the Lord's eyes, just playing God with our salvation?

To take an insult so deep that it shatters any hope of betterment. Such a torment to shatter any belief of salvation when the heart hurts so. Didn't Christ's pain and suffering cover all of ours, or ever so special in our heart? God blesses that person again and again until that person gets the message. God is impartial who is saved. So why rule it for just response?

God Bless Us

We are olden in discrete ways. We learn very oblivious to others. We protect our comfort.
And we are creatures of habits beyond, which we have our fail safer.
And they drag us all, well enough for love, well as bittersweet. Bitter to the quick, sweet to the rest in the Lord. To be one with each other takes time and patience.
The road may be difficult but not lethal.
A kindness is necessary.
Time is the great healer.
Only bitterness can fail one.

The Flesh Stumbles One

Looking beyond oneself is the first step to healing. Then noticing one's flow to be reported as sin.
Overlooking sensitive sensibilities returns bring truth to bear. One may cope well enough on one's own, but the rest see the challenge in Jesus's eyes. To draw closer to Him always provides a better answer. Left to our men and may fail, particularly when two sensitive coping individuals clash with their fleshy humanities.
The flesh needs attention.

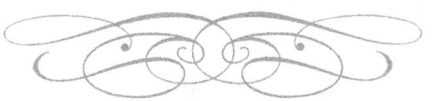

Flaws Temper One

Your wisdom concurs with one's victory. The brighter one is, the brighter the other is.

It all comes down to how well one's relationship is with God and with man. In an ideal atmosphere, both situations should be edified by losses. If it is not the bedrocks of broth situation, then it is a flawed love. One cannot have oneself, as well as these.

One then does not belong but is a loose ranger.

False beliefs, are clings to, are the problem here.

The only answer is to get right with God, first and foremost. Admit one's guilt. He is love.

Championing the Darkness

The most debilitating effect is to have no light in one's candle when a threat is enormous. To have no light burning means you have given upon the Holy Spirit.

This awkwardness comes by profound sinning.

The typical believer has sinning but not to our alarming levels.

When this blasphemy occurs, the fire has long gone out. And instead of blessed graces following one, toxic ones do.

When we no longer marvel at another's championing of an infirmity, we are lost within our own.

Married to God

We are married to Christ by adoption of God. We are His sons and daughters of His kingdom. Like the Body of Christ, we feel each the hurt of one in God.

Grace transfers the hurt or pain in any attack. Until the name of Jesus is uttered, we are all in pain. The graces altogether resonate when the victory cry is made and the sin redeemed. And in the hand of the Redeemer, widow and orphan or married.

And the work of redemption continues until each is married to God.

The Lamb's feast celebrates all such marriages.

Resting in the Spirit

The graces abound in faith. They indicate the depth of friendship with Him. The heart is still forming the image of Christ. It is like a constantly unfinished work of art. But it is in keeping with all practicalities. The faith of one is always being tested for the saving years inherent.

This is where the name of Jesus succeeds the devil.

We must conquer the world and flesh with His hand of righteousness.

It all requires practicing, meeting in His Spirit.

The presence of Him in heaven.

Always in His Kingdom

He is perfect and true. Our confession of sin is brought to His redeeming. And His care is all we receive. All His hosts come to church with Him over me. Grace resounds in me. I am blessed to live for His sake.

The Lord Jesus keeps us in tender care.

He inspires us with the Holy Spirit who enlivens us after redemption where we find ourselves in His kingdom.

We had never left, but the action of a sin clouded our vision.

Each Day

He is asleep, and we are coming. He awakens to our celebration. He says today is the Lord's.
The Lord steps forward in the light. We are reborn in Him.
Abba, thank You, Jesus.
God blesses God for all the good He does. Thank You, Jesus, for all Your good.
Thank You, Holy Spirit.
Pray as I have taught you.
Our Father…
Each day is the Lord God's.

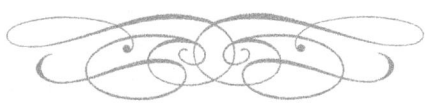

Coping

My nomenclature came as a spiritual language once Christ brought me to spiritual wholeness.

To write it came in a quiet moment in the evening. Before me was a legal pad and a pen. And keeping in mind journaling, I just felt like writing. And so began the whole process. I did not know it would be a healing, a spiritual healing for my affliction, MI.

Now the time is past, and music is my healing, born-again Spirit-led worship music every day.

I know I have my purpose—to help those elder and dear to me.

The healing goes on.

I feel I am healed, as well as in a healing process. It all reflects on my faith in God and family.

The kingdom walk and talk is so essential to the born-again experience. There, there is the sharing of grace and prayer, a working apostolic framework. We are sent to the kingdom for the transforming life.

Now my purpose for my walk here is to be a facilitator for religious faith for the elderly and dear.

Holy Is Your Name

All under grace was holy. This place time with their holiness. God bless.

There are recourses here beyond maintain, of the character and faith of man. The writing is the soul and heart together. Only the Holy Spirit speaks with the marvel of conscience.

The Spirit of God moves one in unknown ways.

The glory of the Holy Spirit confirms His activity. All becomes a part of the consideration.

Every day in Him is new. The peace of Christ recreates.

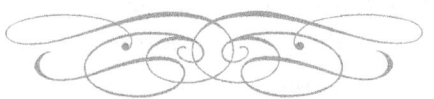

Kingdom Walking

As the evening ebbs, I am rewarded by the sounds of Creation's stirring sounds of the Holy Spirit in concert with the music.

The picture of my mom and I stirs steady grace from me. I know Jesus has my family safe in salvation. This comfort translates to a comfort over decisions. Thank You, Jesus.

Praise be to God on High.

For me, a balance of activity works well.

The coping of my MI has rooted well here with the people and activity present.

Free

It's the esprit de corps of the music I identify with uplift and on to worship. The Father knows the truth of all, Jesus. The Spirit identifies Him, Jesus Christ. The music shows the power therein. Music that worships in praise is the born-again experience. Salvation to all, that is our offering of self, penance restoring the kingdom. It is a rhapsody of shank'n and back'n.

The spirit is alive with Him, resurrected.

Jesus is overcoming one to greater heights.

His name is all the authority we have. In His name, we pray.

Alone Overcome

When I am done for the day, I rest in peace of the Holy Spirit. He is my source to Jesus. My time to reflect is with music, another enabler of the Holy Spirit. I am still a child of God learning the ropes. The DVD uses good repertoires of born-again churches. Altogether, we form the Body of Christ. To have these exponents of Christ singing is reinforcing. It speaks of my station here, follower of love. A day of Pentecost. It is a yes album.

My goals are to be an exemplar of JC.

In Jesus Name

To the weakly guarded, an attack from the demonic may go undetected. It may seem like right out of the blue; small together were called for insult has attacked us.

With our guard down, it's easy to fall in this trap.

Take it to the Lord.

Is this insult true to character of the source?

Is this too flashy a response on our part? Does it justify anger in spite of bless of innocence?

Could this be Satan's sense to discredit a believer and Christmas? Yes, believe in Jesus Christ.

His Sign, Happiness

He gives a notice by the way of a "hubahub" hug that tickles our fancy. It's a sweet'n of our motion. It makes us happy inside. It tells us He is near and in gamesmanship. A little frolic, not flashy because it keeps our thoughts on Him in a pleasant way. He makes us like ourselves by the small innuendos. He makes on us. We call them the calls of inspiration.

God copyrights all He does. We know it is He when Jesus does something, grace is His signature and gifts of the Spirit.

Our will has been maneuvered, our motive is God-centered.

Prayers' Gifts

Prayers are graces among paths in spiritual people. Animals pretend cooperative tones, housed or not, suffer pain.

Faith be led by God, hunger is His talk.

Substance is His result. He sweetens us so for prayer and imagery.

Obligations are covenants of desire. Faith enters desire with God, graces.

Sound carries grace for they faith. No sound is contemplative where He speaks. Music is no sound, meant for faith.

Holiness gifts the maker.

Prayer

Where we put our heads together, only good can come. The only thing that can deter us is our hubris.

With overflowing pride, we are a ready target.

With just the right humility and fear of God, it works.

Fear of God is genuine respect, reverence and awe, of omnipotence and intimate God Spirit.

It is God who answers.

He answers through our graces with each other.

The Habit of Jesus

We are creatures of habit. All habits are hard to loosen or forget. They ultimately refer us to the Savior and to the named life we have with Him. He is the groom, and we are His bride. We are of valor, above murder. We are not totally pure. We are drivers by the prayers of our Lord and Savior Jesus. All He asks of us is to remember Him, met those nasty habits…

Being pure of Jesus is being pure of heart, and the Holy Spirit is the pure overflow.

Purely trusting in the Father is knowing Jesus.

With His

Music keys the heart and the soul. It liberates them. In praise, they work with the mind to elevate Jesus. In worship, oneness with the Maker is achieved. In prayer, He speaks to us.

Music simply makes it easier. It clouds out the distractions. Celebrating Jesus is that way with the worship and praise. Anointed, we wait on the Holy Spirit to key us into the Lord. We are finding the center of His trust, thanking the Father. That is celebration. That is our very being with His.

Baby Lambs

Christmas is one day every day of the year. We wake to each day with a fresh born-again fro for in our heart. Every day is that way, Christ giving Himself over to us in a new way. He does say He makes all things new, including the days of our lives.

Merry Christmas. Every day and to all my dear ones.

You don't have to wait a year to have something new. Celebrate Jesus every day. Merry Christmas. Grow up Christian and be like a child to Him.

Worship the King of Heaven

Glorify His Name. Raise your hearts to taste His goodness. The everlasting salvation is His ultimate healing. We cry from our sin influenced failures to His victory over death. Life that exceeds all dreamt visons of heaven and His kingdom.

We find the very true heart of His in every God blessedness we encounter. Grace over grace guiding us. The Holy Spirit does not lack in graciousness; endless is the hope we have. His faithfulness exceeds all promises in His parables we live out.

Endless Love with Jesus

Thank You, Holy Spirit, for your revelations. God will consume the wrath moment for us so we can do one in all truth. He is risen and restores the Eden of the universe in our kingdom with Him. He is true and forgiving to all come meritoriously to Him, Jesus our God Superior.

Thank You, for Your impeccable goodness was shining through us.

You wait on us endlessly for all calms me.

Jesus, You are unfathomable in Your love for all creation. You are the gift.

Jesus, We Rediscover

God honors those afflicted to Him. Those afflicted seek the Lord, as they see healing from His truth and reward for their afflictions. He afflicts those for His purposes.

He is the Master, Healer. As He uses circumstances to draw us closer to Him, we get to know Him. He uses our desires the same way to born-again moments of our lives. He heals the sore and confused with truth.

He perfects us by staging healing upon us. We discover His personable mercy time and again. We reconsider our views and beliefs to the meritorious nature of His truth.

Thank You, Father

I see the work of Mary and Jesus here. A whole kingdom of God here where I am and where I go. The land of the redeemed.

I find the heart of a sinner confessing in every moment of these diversions, thought running through my mind. Redemption comes with the conscience of the Holy Spirit revealing truth, words of everlasting life.

We become as lambs of God when we take away the sin of another. We are crucified for and until the time of revelation.

Jesus is at the center, the Holy Spirit working.

The kingdom of God is a land of the sinner and the redeemed. Here is a care in print. Jesus is here by the workings of the Holy Spirit.

We are dumb as lambs without the Holy Spirit. With him, we have spiritual gifts and discernment. Sometimes, we have to wait in the Spirit until discernment comes. Otherwise, we fall into the tragedy of judgmentalism.

There, there is shame, guilt, and blame.

Each is a work of God, not in our need of cursing but revelation.

We have each been given a gift of faith from Jesus. He loved us first with agape love, even before our birth.

Christians are many in faith. It is one religion for all believers. Many of faith, sinners and saintly. Some believe saintly ways. Other's belief may margin that belief to sinning more than saintly approaches. The mind decides. The heart is just full of it, sinning or saintly ways.

God is only pleased with us by faith if he has such from us or not. No faith from one keeps one as a work of the prayers and God, unmet.

Kingdom Walking

The heart that receives the words of everlasting life is full of Him.

In that person, the prayers and God have been met. Faith is given unto God, and He is pleased.

The kingdom of God is full of victories and tragedies on that scale. It is a kingdom of hope—hope that Jesus has in all.

The tapestry of life either wears us to Him or not. We either complete Jesus's mission or not for our lives or not. He offers Himself to us. We only have to acknowledge Him. And the kingdom is ours to live out.

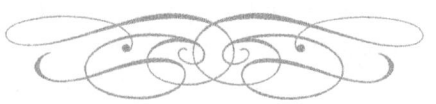

Finding God

I find the course of things strange, get affirming.

It is wholesome, the activity of the Holy Spirit. He inspires courage, that is the face of Jesus. And we shine so when we evangelize our friends. We liberate them to the truth.

When Jesus Christ says His Father is within Him, He is saying that all is within God. God is the knowing of beauty, the truth. The knowing of beauty is love, Jesus Christ. He is, the Father active. The Father is who we are when we know Jesus, the very Son, is before us when we see the Father. It is the universe within faith, all known and unknown; the absolute love, Him.

Celebrate Jesus Every Day, Worship

Whatever you do as a believer, worship Him. Entertain Him. You don't have to have a high IQ, but it shows no IQ not to have time for Him. And if He is your God every day, why not have a faith explosion for Him every day?

Edifying yourself over the Bible only goes so far if you don't see it to thank Jesus. Be born again, not simply born over dull again and again. Wouldn't the Savior like to hear a little more thanks from you instead of just a growing Bible awareness only?

Celebrate the life you have to come into. He has given you a new life in His kingdom. Celebrate it.

Advancing His Name

Oneness is Christ. Jesus leading is trusting the will of the Father.

Actively, we are with the Holy Spirit. In our heart sense, He drives us. His soul is in us, alive. We have come to own it. By heart sense, it moves kingdom-wise. He decorates it, so it is blessed. We shine to glorify His name. The words of truth shape our heart for the coming blessing of grace. We are trusting in His will. Oneness furthers into wholesomeness. Redemption every day.

I can gaze Him in heart by His commingling Spirit, overcoming.

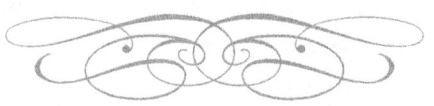

Remember Him

Infused prayers reach the altar of saints in communion, the perfect will of God, after victories of overcoming with the HS inspiration. That is what coming forth from the darkness is.

The more that prayers are focused on Jesus coming through for us, the more infused does the altar of prayer be sensitive to the relationship with God. As the altar becomes infused, we are better joined to God in all respects of prayer and any other way of relationship.

The common basis is the way the altar takes shape by the shared gratefulness. He is so integral to our lives.

An altar to God is a remembrance.

Infused Prayer: Finding His Face to Be Completing Grace

In seeking His face, we find victory and peace four our soul. To Him alone. There, we will find rest for our soul. No more contention with the past but well armored with revelation in the present. God is in control. We surrender.

Absolute surrender follows the dark night, and the night of the senses to be at the center of His will. The transforming summit is there with our image of His Christocentric shining. We have Church before His altar or the communion of saints. The apostolic succession is His perfect will. There is the overcoming victory. The prayers of your heart light up as a candle of constant light. The Holy Spirit remains on you. You are an instrument of His will. The commandments of God are emblazed on your heart.

Sanctifying Life

The dark night is the healing of memories through the presence of God. I am there always within His reconciling in order to see Him. I need His discernment to see the image of God through Him in me shine. It must all reflect the unity of the Holy Spirit. The image or presence is caught up in godly conversation. It is the meeting of God's word and our flesh, transposed to His. That is the reconciliation with. Taking how His flesh would resist sin by the overcoming of praise and worship to God in, about, and through us in faith. The passionate words are the infused prayers that we recall God sanctifying the experience told. And then we recognize God was then as now always there.

Infused Prayer

Naming someone in a jeer is to desire a better hold of toxic categories. One seems like a threat. To get beyond this is love.
All is quenched in love.
To the mind/heart paradox, love heals the straight by prayer. Worship turns the mind to the heart. Once again saved by His greatness.
And we are imbued with wonder, limitless God. Alleluia.
He is and we are that love is forgiving and limitless. Only a few forsake heaven for themselves in view for their only love for, to, and about themselves.

Number Two

Expository writing is all I do. I expose the heart and spirit by discernment. All it requires is a vex upon my soul.
From what I am able to write is that all is perfectly reconciled to good order and peace.
It is the lack or overabundance of peace I write about.

Prayer of the heart is like discursively revealing the missing piece to a mindset jigsaw puzzle. It is a spontaneous prayer. In this case, I see nothing missing.

Racism or other isms are attempts by the cowardly to ignore some folks, putting others in a toxic category.

Number Three

In the goings of things comes the point—the point of why things were done at all. The point of gratitude can answer all.

Gratitude tells all things are clear and operative to the good. The past has been reconciled to the present. Now reconcile yourself further ahead. Interpreting what will happen with these legal maneuvers is guesswork. And what will come down as a result of said decisions is up in the air. But a result likely will be a restrictive mandate, strangling the economy and worse. The timing will be scheduled. By winter's end, we should be free of this virus.

The Transforming Summit Is Key

Charismatic music tries to imitate the Lord in performance of the milestones of the Lord, infused prayer. Just like the title to pages is meant to awaken a character or attitude in the Lord's kingdom. It is simply the start of infused prayer leading me through a contemplative experience, a reward for taking in the experiential Lord. How personable He is.

And yet none of this may occur because you are ghost that point in the transforming summit.

Altars to the Lord

Infused prayers are like charged recollections of the Lord that happen in real time. Contemplative prayer incubates this infused nature of such experiential prayers. Called by the HS in this deeply heartened faith, one is with Christ. Special graces accompany such a visit. One's attention is on Jesus and His entreating.

It all starts with Abba Father through Jesus. And Jesus through the HS and faith in HS.

Music can inspire such depictions. But it is too fast without repetitions. In this case, an iron of the Lord can be valuable and not the faces of the singers and musicians.

Most important are those milestones of infused prayer where He is.

Infused Prayer and Scripture

Scripture is what infused prayer is with the inspiration of the HS. The gifting of grace is what the apostles had with the direct experience of the Lord, with the believer's graces and His graces affected.

Contemplative and the HS's powers as the Spirit of truth enabled the writers of the Gospels to write the Gospels. The contemplative prayer became infused prayer for the apostles because they experienced the Lord and the apostles' inspiration over His time with them.

Infused prayer requires a real experience of Jesus Christ through the HS. In a contemplative means, the prayers over a real experience of Jesus, evoked by the HS, have an infused nature. It means where in life you experience Jesus or discover parallels of Jesus in scripture you have contemplative infused prayers with Him.

Journals, Altars Given to Christ

So the thing to do is to make an altar of prayer when we know of Him. So doing, the vivid experience of God becomes infused prayer we know God through and deepen our relationship of Him by.

Contemplative becomes as we resort to this source of infused prayer.

So first, depict in our discernment when we actually felt His experience as we sensed it. Maybe there were several events. Try placing scripture to the prayer, preferable of Jesus's life and allow graces to form the prayer. It's the same way the Gospels were formed and journaling is.

Love Songs/Music

Love songs spur the viable heart and spirit. Until the HS comes to one, the spirit of men could be considered so empty that love had no place in it. It was dead. And the heart was not viable. It was evil because it draws its strength from circumstances, not a holy God.

We were in chains to the earth, Satan's stronghold, before Jesus came in the flesh, salvation.

It is His Spirit now that keeps the heart with love songs sourced from Scripture.

Love songs meld the heart and encourage the spirit to seek the Spirit connection and not mere circumstances of earthly secular origin.

Then we know the HS, the mind of Christ reflects in us.

Good Heroic Virtue

It would seem that order is a necessity. HS is calling for meditated writing. Choose God centering abiding.

His will puts all in alignment. Pray. Surrender. Let Him abide in worship. Victory for the kingdom, ever expanding truth.

The Christ is the universe. The expansion of inspiration for those in Him. All creativity is in the HS. He is the life in Christ. Jesus is the Truth, Life, and Way. Only through Him can one come to the Father, Abba.

You in Christ experience all inspiration toward the Jesus Christ you could wish to pray for, the imaging of God completed in Spirit, the church and the Groom. He is yours in totality, if this is the altar of infused prayer, Scripture.

You exist as the gospel, your heroic virtue.

Loving Contacts

This place is a schema word for love.

It goes without saying there are many beautiful people and their relationships in this kingdom of the Lord. As with all kingdoms of the Lord, the believer's heart is in constant meditation and praise.

The Lord rules with sweet and deep love that people here surrender to. The Lord supplies a group that we can extend from. God bless we have such a personal Lord. He is the all in all.

It is important to gather a few good contacts and keep in communal contacts here to keep prayer alive and ongoing.

Change

The conversation down the hallway and the noise above my apartment all tell to the healthy life in this retirement place.

There is a comfortable peace about this. The seasons long for winter here.

The TV and I are partners. The rest fell into place. God is here in His faithful. Seeing Him in His faithful in seeing Him face to face. There is no one like Him.

The audio of the DVD definitely puts God in the good light. Altogether, the DVD is lifted. It is old Pentecostal.

Coming into the light is a marvelous pursuit. The truth always sets me free to the call of holiness. At the center is Jesus the Christ, HS, and Abba the Father as God. We stand in all faith in love. We know Him because we are changed.

Conrad 2

The residents here have the chance to fulfill their faith ambitions.
We are safe and alive in a community.
My Jesus Christ lives well respected here.
The apartment facilitates me well. The extended future is dubious. Here in the now, I am able to think clearly. My pursuits are simple.

In fact, most pursuits are neutralized with nowhere to go. I just guess they just satisfy me, what they are meant to do, with no further purpose, I guess. I think there is some causal result outside of myself.

My desire is journaling and prayer to follow this worship DVD, as well as a production of cards. A portfolio. A stamp collection. A balance routine. A good waking hour and study.

Conrad 1

The HS consumes one in a place like this. All thoughts on memories become reconciled. The sounds and texture of daily habits leave an unmistakable groove within the spirit. It is here the HS blesses, so freedom is enacted and not self-imposed slavery. In this way, each day is brand-new to experience on all levels.

The HS leads one past ruts to victories in grace, past legal suits. The heart has the chance to fully breathe altogether newness of a day.

The HS deepens its control by inspiring discernment. Here, the heart takes in healing to reconcile it to God's will.

Mercy Me

Your very hand upon me coaxes me to tether to your commands of love. My conscience yields its portion like a fresh shower rinses my body. The words of the gospel are as new as the dew that harbors moisture.

All my thoughts indicate my cooperation with the touches of the Holy Spirit. My workings of pen are out of an unblemished day within my wholesomeness. I spring anew this day because all is within His command and control.

I rest in His creativeness knowing full well all is well because of faith—faith that burns the cries of peace within me. I am taken to shock to witness His mercy for me.

HS Control in Prayer

To reconcile perfectly with the HS is to reconcile across faith in Jesus. Then everything comes true for His will in plan and purpose for the believer. Sometimes, it requires repetitive prayer to express the heartfelt need despite what strongholds are in the mind working satanically. Scripture can help, centered on the healing power of love.

Some groans and heaving sounds will artifice thoughts no longer in strongholds but grace. It is an inspired activity. The HS will indicate what is necessary.

Rapture in the Light

The book of Revelation is completed in each, as the heart shines to light the mind. Jesus Christ is imaged.

His resurrection comes as each accepts the baptism of the Holy Spirit. Each comes to heroic generosity as it is fulfilled.

The words of refreshment are coming, the more the HS discerns with me.

It is otherworldly that drives me. Praise God. All Jesus, HS.

The playing of the music allows the HS to have a pulpit of light on us. The anointing is transferable. The anointing reflects the summing of infused prayer, all from Christ's inspiration.

As we shine, the rapture completes us.

Walking

I have seen life rewards. It rewards when less likely. It is the doings of the Lord.

Our challenge is our nearsightedness. Vision only comes with the humble acceptance of Him.

A chapter of life ends when all give up their attachments to a material that became more an icon than a means to further life.

The test of us is whether we can walk on with all our frailties past disaster to a better living of those frailties. We are all made up by frailties that get tested always for wholesomeness. Finally, when all is lost, do we listen to God telling us to trust Him explicitly?

Branching Out

Back in the 1940s, I wrote many pages of heart. Yes, I was a new convert to my chosen faith. I was inspired to journal faith. Now I am sure to look at contemplative holiness.

It resides in all of us by the mystery of faith in Christ here at the Conrad. Holiness in the Father is wholeness through Christ, the template of all forgiveness. It requires an emptying of all bias to allow strict natures to be seen wounded. Woundedness arrives in one when "artificing" life to created objects takes place, denoting viral objects less of life's rewards. It is making an icon a god figure, not the magisterium of Christ. Holiness is not true to the Godhead, but instead iconographic wholeness takes place in one. This is the antithesis to the real wholeness.

The Way

God is perfect holiness, while I am in His holiness discerning better to it. It is the call of being anew in Him. Before was the perfecting hope in Him. Now, in time, in His call to be in Him for His holiness to be my perfecting not by mine. Humility is His prayer in me. All comes to Him in due fashion.

As I discern, the folly of people's free will is played out in me.

It comes to me, the rebellions spiritual warfare of both ends.

Jesus, played out, is not heard.

Jesus left the temple as the glory was gone. Abba Father leads us.

Praise God in His holiness, make us whole again. Be sure of Him in loving truth to trust in Him.

Scriptural Beginnings

Infused prayer is like the deepest recollection of something. Instead, it is not just a live memory, but also a condition of discernment you know Jesus. You experience His real person is intermixed with your prayer. It happens when we seek deeper abiding. It is common in scripture reading and worship. Can you imagine how touched they were by Jesus and moved in the spirit by the Holy Spirit to write the Gospel? I came I hope you can too! Discerned love in prayer.

Inspiration Is Christ

The wholeness of faith and the inspiration of infused prayer is Christ, His gifting to the believer. The change into light couples with the heart given to charismatic senses and HS controlling.

It is all kingdom. We are forever His children. It all comes to emptying oneself of attachments and having dark night.

Mark 10:15–16.

First John 3:10.

To purify is to pray. To this end, we are singing songs of Jesus.

Lessons to learn are not first little and cooperatives.

I battle the carnal with food.

My battle is neutral.

Wholeness

The battle of the mind is for true wholeness, contemplative infused prayer. It is gifting as a reward for readiness.

Wholeness deflects the simpleton's heart cry. It is a broken one relying upon wit, not inspired love. Here, we call the stiff-necked one. Once broken, now healed in Christ, we seek His wholeness with the Father. We gave into righteousness through Jesus. We gain into Christly wholeness through the Father.

The gifting of faith readies us for holiness, the gifting of wholeness.

The church of believers is blessed by wholeness. The kingdom encapsulates all who come to Christly ways.

The soft ways are the readiness of faith. Pride exceeds and fallen.

Prayer

Jesus is the center of my Church, as Mary is the epitome of the believer. She, as any of us, indicates when He is to act many prayers. Only He acts in cooperation upon them. He mediates as she does, and we do as well. The guiding humility in all to prayers is key to God making communion over all therein. It is Him seeing Himself, the Christ that makes away to the life and truth of prayers realized. In this way, it reflects His Gospel power of resurrection and redemption in salvation. Apostolic in nature is the infinitive closeness His marriage is to the Church. One realizes himself in the kingdom of God as a child. My pathway is a rearing in worship.

The Way

We alternately wear the face of Christ. It is our shining of the Church and the Holy One. Every day, we shine for Jesus. We follow the Marian cult as an example to holiness. Humble celebration and prayer make the realization of Christ and the Church. It is a contemplative prayer. Christ is the mystic to us children of God. When we admit to being in the kingdom, all is mystic contemplation.

Each of us is in a gathering phase. Sharing if need be to truth. The presence of God is a pleasure in all graces.

My hope is to beacon grace. It is such a pleasure we are in that we find His wishes a pleasure.

Christ Is

Deep conversion is contemplative prayer, responsible mysticism. It means delegating a means to Christ and the marriage. A born-again spirit man can lead into such humility. Repentance is life to the Godhead.

The marriage is when we see Christ face to face in us. The heart, soul, and mind mirror Him alive. In Christ, we are His face. His face is all of us caught up in the Spirit of God.

He moves, He speaks, he is among us, the soul of God resurrected through new living of life. The mystic life is caught up in mystery that answers all of us in Christ. Answers in Christ are the means of conversion.

Christocentric

Politics is always off the edge that is how they make a difference in candidate vote. Democracy is a golden rule. Sports is a rule for the stars. It is the where with all that makes relationship what is always a victory in Christ. Relationship is conviction and conversion to ideal ways.

The present ideal is Christ. To emanate grace like His. To fill His church so being.

Today is no exception, forgiveness is the rule. It is the template for all relationships, lost and new. As all are found saved and burned out beyond recognition. Take what you can and go on with new life. A place is a word unless there is our living.

His Way

It's too early to start abiding old relationships when you are in the flux of change.

Change is a good breath to the soul. Change is a meter of good mental health. Change is a way within that actuates one on the outside.

The features may be pretty. But they really sour out.

The Way of God is Truth for the Life we find by living.

Epworth will not resurrect for the voices, but life will always be found in Christ, as a new day is found in the ashes of the old. Kindness is a factor we often omit for the expedience of living life fall. We see a fullness but not its lackings.

Moment to Moment

To commune as the apostles did around Jesus is to admit our humble roots of faith, so richly preserved through time and prayers. The match of prayer elevates our concerns to His control.

To catch the virosome nature of God is to make the inspired word your life, soul, and meaning. We look deeper and find He matches us with every turn with the strength of inspiration for infused prayer.

Infused prayer is at the heart of the response of the Maker to our petitions.

I feel I write in moments and not as well. Infused prayer is what the gospel writings all come from.

Each Day in Christ

Each day have to wonder why it all came this way. I have to admit in the center of His will lies the center of His pleasure for Him and us. He pleasures us, so in peace, we want to pleasure Him.

In Christ, we have no desire but Him and His people reflect Him. We seek the true God, Jesus Christ. The triune love spells us. The Holy Spirit is alive and active. And we are blessed.

The shadow of God lies in His shadow; there was living sacrifice, not truly abiding with Him for we have a penance to serve.

His peace begs our spirit to come in. The HS says we are not ready. Infused prayer has not been lived out, perfect scripture.

Salvation Is Today

I hear the DVD for the untold time. Coffee and water wait. I am settled into His way. It is all inspiration this Christ. I breathe knowing full well my hobbies are in good stead. The DVD plays "God Is Here," and He is triune in all respect, keeping me well. He reminds me the people here are the children of His kingdom in need of intercession, which I often in Spirit and the truth of His name. The DVD continues with the endless worship experience. It is well in my spirit to know He abides. I discern the growth today here. My faith is boundless for the people here.

Discerning

I carry the beat of the music into worship. I know He is because my soul dances. I think of the time, and it waits on the music. My spirit is lifted to discern. I think of infused prayer, and this is it. To set a bedrock of prayerful discerning to continue to build there in an inspired worship. That is scripture for Christ, as it was built. Years of meditating on the actual experience when He was here to build an altar of prayer called the Gospel. Only in a small way I do this on my life. I do not have holy discerning.

All Within His Hand

My article of faith hinges with the Lord. He is all consuming greatness. Nothing is amiss. All is within His grasp. His grip spells the beginning of a new day—a day of grandeur and intimate natures. He rules me severely and with ownership. I am poised for all expedience to graft grass into any dialogue. Whether it be real or my reach in sport, He grants me wholesomeness. To empty my selflessness for His.

My establishment each day is to erect a tall tower in His name. It is a tower of His everlasting goodness to me and all who believe. We believe in the unconquerable spirit of God. He has decided all that pertain to life, He controls all manner of desire and whim to excel.

Fulfilling Jesus Time

The matchup counted have been anywhere but in heaven. The present is new, for the future is whatever hope you want to realize. It's all up to you to make the day whatever you wish.

It's like a ready-made comfort home with a slew of good neighboring people, all made up with good motives.

Free is your time to fill in.

For me, it is a blended time. One with one friend, then another. Making sure of time spent alone the quality time. Attempting to better wake-up time.

One thing to keep hold of is the play of relationships. Always to Christ-centered pursuits. Deeper in Him with abiding and abiding partners.

The Healer

Speak of your day. What do you worship? What do you think keeps your day?

Is it touched? Or are you the sole element? Do you see where it goes? Is God real for you? What externally do you need to happen? Are you healed?

Here you find the healer. Mind, body, and soul.

This Brevailer is an all satisfactory health campus. Depending on the need and ability one is situated. In the situation came appropriate freedom and responsibility. Brevailer is the healer.

The wholesomeness is Jesus Christ. Purification and better abiding leads one further in His mystery. It is in all relationships so effected, the cold of holiness.

This is salvation.

Infused Journaling

A fall from grace may depict a timing for retreat. And once that retreat is made to continue anew with journaling and a new sense of reconciliation.

Prayers from heaven are a series of writings on first impressions to the Gospels.

The personable Lord is an index to His way in journaling.

And from a fall comes the prayers of promise, the Our Father, the glory be to the Father, come Holy Spirit, come Holy Ghost, and the Apostles' Creed.

The writings on infused prayer are transitory to a new journaling.

No One Like Jesus

My practice is to remain within His will for me. That means die, sing my prayer practice for Him. My entirety is devoted so. How He plans furthering my time with you, I don't know. I do see you are a devote believer. I am too. I know there are ways and means to this; I am just a pioneer.

This has to effect a deeper time with Him. Right now, I confer with you, the deacon. We are just beginning to delve into source material. A richer, deeper relationship is the goal. More focused. I have a charismatic background, which I hope does not upset you. Remember, all things are possible through God.

A Day

The people here are apostolic in their mission of life. The each have a message in their final place to be sent to. It is biblical, their account. It amounts to what kind of spirit they possess and the spirituality to it. I am only account to mine. Stamps, news, stocks, music, and prayer seem to top the list. Food and meals buttress it up. Sleep heals all. Hydration is core. The phone and computer are obscure. I try to keep up the friendships and group activities, as well as my writing and TV.

My time is over and my wishes are to read. I find and seek what would make satisfaction.

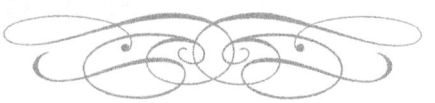

About the Author

Peter Boice grew up in Erie, Pennsylvania. He was a church boy for years, with no personal relationship. It was not until circumstances caught up in me that he began seeking Him. He had totaled several cars, failed twice at college, committed suicide, and had mental health recovery since age twenty-one. Finally, at age thirty-five, after being disabled from a career in machining did he seek the Lord. He went from an Episcopal church to a First Assembly of God. At that Pentecostal church, he found a personal relationship with God. There, he was given an adult baptism at age thirty-eight. He learned of the baptism of the Holy Spirit. He felt bad to enter a Life in the Spirit Seminar. There, he received the baptism and became a charismatic Catholic. He then entered a charismatic Catholic prayer group, Light in the World. He became part of a charismatic church, Bread of Life. All of this followed being saved on December 18, 1989, in the back of a faith-believing bookstore. He, in being charismatic, gained into writing discernments. Here are some.

Printed in the USA
CPSIA information can be obtained
at www.ICGtesting.com
JSHW080235070224
56692JS00001B/23